Worship, Watch, and Warn

Worship, Watch, and Warn
The Revelation
of Jesus Christ

This inductive Bible study is designed for individual, small group, or classroom use. A leader's guide with full lesson plans and the answers to the Bible study questions is available from Regular Baptist Press. Order RBP0056 online at www.regularbaptistpress.org, e-mail orders@rbpstore.org, call toll-free 1-800-727-4440, or contact your distributor.

REGULAR BAPTIST PRESS
1300 North Meacham Road
Schaumburg, Illinois 60173-4806

The Doctrinal Basis of Our Curriculum

A more detailed statement with references is available upon request.

- The verbal, plenary inspiration of the Scriptures
- Only one true God
- The Trinity of the Godhead
- The Holy Spirit and His ministry
- The personality of Satan
- The Genesis account of creation
- Original sin and the fall of man
- The virgin birth of Christ
- Salvation through faith in the shed blood of Christ
- The bodily resurrection and priesthood of Christ
- Grace and the new birth
- Justification by faith
- Sanctification of the believer

- The security of the believer
- The church
- The ordinances of the local church: baptism by immersion and the Lord's Supper
- Biblical separation— ecclesiastical and personal
- Obedience to civil government
- The place of Israel
- The pretribulation rapture of the church
- The premillennial return of Christ
- The millennial reign of Christ
- Eternal glory in Heaven for the righteous
- Eternal torment in Hell for the wicked

WORSHIP, WATCH, AND WARN: THE REVELATION OF JESUS CHRIST
Adult Bible Study Book
Vol. 60, No. 2
© 2011
Regular Baptist Press • Schaumburg, Illinois
www.regularbaptistpress.org • 1-800-727-4440
Printed in U.S.A.
All rights reserved
RBP0059 • ISBN: 978-1-60776-498-4

Contents

Preface

The book of Revelation is a fascinating look into the future, which is filled with both sobering and joyous times. Our responses to the book could be many, but we can summarize them in three words: *Worship, Watch, and Warn*. Worship Christ as He is revealed in the book. Watch for His coming by serving Him. Warn the lost of God's impending judgment.

As you study this book you will sense the Holy Spirit directing you to respond in these three ways. That is what God intended. John even included a message to the reader in the opening verses of the book. He tells us that the person who reads the book and keeps those things written in it will be blessed (Rev. 1:3).

So approach this study with more than an interest in learning how to navigate through the complicated passages in Revelation. Prepare your heart to respond to the Spirit. Let God's Word work in your heart. Impress upon yourself that the book of Revelation is a necessary study for a proper development of the spiritual life (2 Tim. 3:16, 17).

The Vision of Christ

The revelation of Jesus Christ demands we worship Him, watch for His coming, and warn the lost of coming judgment.

Revelation 1

"I am he that liveth, and was dead; and, behold, I am alive for evermore, Amen; and have the keys of hell and of death" (Revelation 1:18).

Benjamin Franklin is well known to Americans as a student of electricity and an inventor. His inventions include the lightening rod, the Franklin stove, and even bifocal glasses. What his autobiography (*The Autobiography of Benjamin Franklin*) makes clear—and what might surprise many Americans today—is that Franklin did not patent his inventions. He believed that "as we enjoy great advantages from the inventions of others, we should be glad of an opportunity to serve others by any invention of ours; and this we should do freely and generously."

Getting Started

1. What is something you could reveal about yourself that others would be surprised to learn?

2. How might people react to your revelation?

3. How might your life be different if God hadn't given us the book of Revelation as a way to learn more about Christ?

The book of Revelation reveals Christ to us. We should respond to Christ's revelation of Himself by worshiping Him, watching for His return, and warning the lost of coming judgment.

Searching the Scriptures

Revelation 1 provides a fitting introduction to the entire book. It contains the key to the three major divisions (1:19), and it explains the reason the book was written (1:9–11).

The Revelation of Jesus Christ

The opening words of verse 1 give the true title of this writing: "The Revelation of Jesus Christ." He is both its source and its subject. It came from Him (22:16) and manifests Him. The translation "revelation" is based upon a word transliterated as "apocalypse." It means "to uncover, to unveil, or to lay bare." It thus stresses a disclosure for the purpose of understanding, not a covering up in secrecy.

The cover of this study has a curtain being pulled back. That is the idea of Revelation. A curtain is pulled back in a sense so we can better understand Christ, including His plans for the future.

4. Why is it important to know that the book of Revelation is Christ's revelation of Himself?

5. How should knowing this affect the way you read the book?

Sequence of Transmission

The sequence of transmission is clearly presented in verses 1–3. The content of the book of Revelation was given to Christ by God the Father within the redemptive program. Christ then sent His angel to John (1:1; 22:16). The means of communication to John is indicated by the verb "signified" (1:1), a reference to symbolic visions that manifest spiritual significance.

The purpose of the revelatory sequence was "to shew unto his servants things which must shortly come to pass" (1:1). God has sovereignly determined the end of this time-space universe and the means to that end (Dan. 2:21; Eph. 1:11). He also has chosen to reveal these truths to His servants, people such as John and the keepers of the book (cf. Amos 3:7).

6. Why could we say that Christ's revelation of His judgment on the lost demonstrates His grace?

Blessings of Revelation

Revelation is the only book of Scripture that begins with a direct promise of blessing for the actual reading of its contents. In fact, seven special blessings recorded within its pages. "He that readeth" (note the singular) refers to that individual who actually read the original manuscript in each church; whereas "they that hear" (plural) are the members of the churches who heard the oral reading. In application, all believers today have the individual and corporate privilege and blessing to read, to hear, and to keep the spiritual content of the book.

7. What does this blessing imply about the possibility of understanding the book of Revelation?

Greetings

In his greeting John addressed seven churches of the Roman province of Asia (1:4) that were probably founded as the result of Paul's ministry in Ephesus. He passed along greetings from the Trinity.

God the Father is described as the One "which is, and which was, and which is to come" (Rev. 1:4). These three aspects of time show His timelessness or His eternal nature.

God the Spirit is designated as "the seven Spirits". This unique title probably refers to His sevenfold or total perfection.

God the Son, Jesus Christ, is identified in three ways (1:5). He is "the faithful witness." Christ perfectly revealed God in what He said, did, and was. He is also "the first begotten of the dead." Christ demonstrated His priestly function in His sacrificial death and subsequent resurrection. He became the first to receive an immortal, incorruptible resurrection body. And Christ is "the prince of the kings of the earth." He is the sovereign Who will assert His kingly prerogatives when He returns to the earth.

8. What do these identifications of Christ mean to you? Choose one word for each of the three identifications.

What Christ Has Done

John dedicated the book to Christ because of His spiritual accomplishments, His future glory, and His present sovereignty.

Christ loved us so much that He died for us (Rev. 1:5). Although John's emphasis here is upon the sacrificial act manifested at Calvary, that type of love goes on forever (Rom. 8:35–39).

Christ "washed us from our sins in his own blood" (Rev. 1:5b). The spiritual washing of regeneration removed the guilt, penalty, and actual sins so that the child of God is spiritually clean before God. The means of cleansing is the shed blood of Christ.

Christ has constituted believers as "kings" (Rev. 1:6). Not only are they in the spiritual kingdom of God, but also they will rule over the earthly kingdom when Christ returns to the earth to establish that theocracy.

Christ has also made His own to become priests (1:6). They are a holy and royal priesthood.

As a response to what Christ has done, believers should render glory and dominion to Him (1:6). To glorify Christ is to acknowledge Him to be what He is and to manifest in one's personal life those spiritual qualities that correspond to Him.

9. Read Revelation 1:5b, 6. How does what Christ has done impact your life?

What Christ Will Do

Verse seven refers to Christ's future return to earth after the Tribulation. The verse does not refer to the rapture of the Church before the Tribulation. Christ will be seen by both the living saved and the living unsaved when He descends to the earth. The two major groups of humanity will also see Him. The nation of Israel is seen as those "which pierced him" (cf. John 19:34–37; 20:25, 27). The Gentile nations, the other major people group, are included in the phrase "all kindreds of the earth."

Who Christ Is

Verse eight includes descriptions of Who Christ is. He is the Alpha and Omega (Rev. 1:8). These two names stand for the first and the last letters of the Greek alphabet. Christ is the sum total—the beginning and completion—of all that could be said or written about the essence of God.

Christ is also eternal and self-existent, qualities seen in the titles "the beginning and the ending" and "which is, and which was, and which is to come" (1:8).

Christ's title "the Almighty" points to His sovereignty (1:8). He can work in and through the activities of men and nations, both good and evil, to accomplish His ultimate purpose—the glorification of God and the blessing of His people.

10. What does this dedication of the book to Christ remind you about the completeness of His work?

John's Condition

Although John was a revered apostle, he simply named himself as his readers' brother in the family of God. He was also their companion in tribulation, in the Kingdom, and in the patience of Jesus Christ (1:9).

John described his banishment to the island of Patmos in the Aegean Sea by the emperor Domitian (1:9). John stated two reasons for his exile—his commitment to the truth of the Word of God and his witness for Christ.

11. Read Revelation 1:9. How well was John doing at worshiping, watching, and warning?

John set forth his prophetic experience. He literally "came to be in the Spirit" (1:10). This later occurred when John was caught up into Heaven (4:2). In this vehicle of Spirit control, John could be transported into future time and space to see and to receive special revelation.

Vision of Christ

John heard the voice of Christ, a sound as loud and clear as a trumpet (1:10). Christ commanded John to "write" and to "send." The book of Revelation is the written record of what John was about to see. The apostle then was to send the finished volume to the seven churches of Asia.

John turned around to see the person Who had just spoken to him.

He first saw the seven golden candlesticks or lampstands, but subsequently he perceived Christ in the midst of them (1:12).

In typology, the Jewish lampstand prefigured the Messiah, the light of His people (John 1:4). The seven golden candlesticks that John saw symbolize the seven local churches of Asia. The vision thus represented Christ, in all of His moral and resurrection glory, about to pronounce a spiritual evaluation of the churches over which He is the authoritative head.

The Description

12. Read Revelation 1:13–16. Which description of Christ in this passage is most striking to you?

Christ often referred to Himself as the Son of Man. This title designated His humanity and His redemptive, Messianic function. His full-length garment resembles the type worn by the Old Testament priest-judge (Exod. 28:2). The high priest had golden thread within his girdle, but the breastplate of Christ is solid gold. It probably symbolizes His worth and royalty.

The whiteness of His head and hairs seems to portray His eternity, purity, wisdom, and deity (1:14). The eyes of fire speak of perfect discernment.

The feet of brass possibly represent Christ's pure, righteous judgment (1:15). He is no respecter of persons or churches. The voice of many waters depicts the authority and power of His spoken word.

In Christ's right hand are seven stars (1:16). The seven stars are later identified as "the angels of the seven churches" (1:20). The Greek word for "angels" literally means "messengers." Some view these stars as the guardian angels of the churches. Since angels minister to individual believers, it is possible that they could attend the activities of believers joined together in local churches. Others regard the stars as the human messengers, even the pastors of the churches.

The two-edged sword out of Christ's mouth portrays His Word, which applies both to the saved and the unsaved (1:16). With it, He can chastise His own people (2:12, 16) or smite the wicked nations at Armageddon (19:15, 21).

The shining of Christ's countenance as the sun represents the glory of His deity (1:16). Isaiah saw this glory even before God the Son became incarnate (Isa. 6:1–8).

13. Which of the descriptions of Christ in Revelation 1:12–16 might believers today need to be reminded of the most?

14. Which description do you need to be reminded of the most?

The Response

John's response to the sight of Christ was dramatic. He fell at Christ's feet as if he was dead (1:17).

15. Read Revelation 1:17a. Why would John fall at Christ's feet as if he was dead?

16. Do you think your response would be any different? Explain.

Our mortal finiteness and our falling short of Christ's glory overwhelm us in His presence. Christ ministered to John by touching the apostle and by speaking to him regarding His titles.

The self-revelation of the Savior through the titles shows His relationships to time and eternity and to death and life.

17. Read Revelation 1:17b, 18. Why would Christ's titles in these verses be particularly encouraging to John?

The title "the first and the last" indicates Christ's deity (1:17). He is Jehovah God. The next title, "and was dead" affirms His humanity (1:18). Christ took to Himself a complete humanity through the virgin conception and birth. As a divine-human person, He experienced death on the cross but then overcame death through His resurrection.

Through His death and resurrection, He destroyed Satan. He has the keys, the authority, over those who are in Hades (Hell) and over death. Hades is the place where the soul of the unsaved goes at death, and death is the realm of the body. At the Great White Throne Judgment, Christ will call the unsaved out of death and Hell to appear before Him (Rev. 20:11–15).

The Command to Write

Revelation 1:19 is the key to the major divisions of the book. John had just seen the vision of Christ (Rev. 1). Christ would later show John "the things which must be hereafter" (4:1—22:5). Thus, "the things which are" must be the seven letters to the seven churches (Rev. 2; 3).

From this opening chapter we know how John came to write down the prophecies contained in this Book. We know its structure and that it reveals things yet to come. In its revelation of Jesus Christ and its unfolding of events yet future it is a source of special comfort and guidance in these days that precede His return.

18. Record key phrases from Revelation 1 that call you to worship Christ, watch for His coming, or warn the unsaved of coming judgment.

Making It Personal

19. What one or two impressions about Christ does Revelation 1 leave in your mind?

20. What changes should those impressions make in your life?

21. What specific responses should you make in light of the revelation of Christ in Revelation 1?

22. Memorize Revelation 1:18.

The Seven Churches, Part 1

Christ knows what is good and what is bad in each local church and what each church must do to be pleasing to Him.

Revelation 2

"Nevertheless I have somewhat against thee, because thou hast left thy first love" (Revelation 2:4).

E ngland takes great care in preserving their historical churches—the buildings that is. Beginning by at least 1605, laws were put into place by the Church of England to ensure regular inspections of their church buildings. England is now filled with well-preserved churches that serve as national landmarks instead of places of worship. Local committees are responsible for raising most of the funds—around 110 million pounds a year. Had as much care been given to what Christ thought of the church people, the nation no doubt would be better off.

Getting Started

1. If Christ came to your church, what do you think would be on His evaluation list?

2. What sorts of things might Christ pay little or no attention to?

Christ will never physically visit your church, but He is still the evaluator of it. Christ, as head of the church, discerns, judges, and supports each local church.

Christ gives an evaluation of seven churches in Revelation 2 and 3. This lesson will examine four of those evaluations.

Searching the Scriptures

The seven letters all follow a similar literary format. Each contains an address, a description of Christ, a commendation of works, a complaint against error, an exhortation to repent, a warning for disobedience, a promise to the overcomer, and an instruction to all churches.

The Letter to Ephesus

Ephesus was the most prominent city in the Roman province of Asia. Its population was about 250,000 in the first century. Paul established the church there during his third missionary journey (Acts 19).

Christ described Himself to Ephesus as the One "that holdeth the seven stars in his right hand" (Rev. 2:1). The vision of Christ in Revelation 1:16 indicated that Christ "had" the stars, but here He "holds" them. "Having" indicates possession; whereas holding indicates protection. As the living Head of the church, Christ holds, controls, and protects the pastors whom He has given to local churches.

3. Read Revelation 2:1. How should the picture of Christ in this verse affect the way you treat and respond to your pastor?

Christ portrayed Himself as walking among the churches. This action suggests that He was reviewing them, as a general with his troops. He was analyzing their spiritual condition and their capacity to bear light.

4. What thoughts come to your mind when you consider Christ as a general inspecting your church, His troops?

Christ commended the Ephesian church in six areas (Revelation 2:2–4, 6). First, the believers' labor involved not only what they did, but also the effort and toil expended. Second, the believers had patiently endured persecutions and trials. Third, they were rightfully intolerant of moral evil and sinful men. Fourth, they had discernment to perceive doctrinal apostates and had exposed their false apostolic credentials. Fifth, they had not fainted or quit in the midst of severe pressure. Sixth, they hated the deeds of the Nicolaitanes.

5. Read Revelation 2:4. What might be some clues that a church is performing duties without love?

6. What might be a remedy for losing one's first love?

Christ registered only one complaint against Ephesus. The church performed its duties apart from love (2:4). The main motivation in Christian living must be a love for Christ (2 Cor. 5:14).

7. Read 1 Corinthians 13:1–3. What good is your service for God if you do it without love?

Christ gave three commands to the church at Ephesus: remember, repent, and do. The commands relate to the past, present, and future (Rev. 2:5). The Ephesians' "first works" were works saturated with a love for the Savior and for His people. The Ephesians needed to remember what their service for the Lord used to be like.

The believers at Ephesus then needed to repent, or to want to change their thinking. They needed to hate what they had become.

8. What "loves" might a believer need to repent of in order to make room for loving Christ again?

Finally, the Ephesians had to serve Christ out of love for Him once again. Christ demanded action once the Ephesians realized their lack of love.

The warning in verse 5 does not suggest the loss of personal salvation for individual disobedience, but rather the removal of corporate privilege and responsibility to serve the Lord. The candlestick represented the effective witness of the total church.

The promise in verse 7 was to the individual believer within the church. The title "overcomer" does not refer to the obedient Christian within the church who follows the three commands; rather, it is a synonym for the genuine child of God. Regardless of what happens to the corporate structure of the local church, the individual believer is promised eternal access to the tree of life (Rev. 22:2). He or she has guaranteed deliverance from the effects of both physical and spiritual death.

The Letter to Smyrna

Smyrna was a wealthy seaport about thirty-five miles north of Ephesus. The city is mentioned only here in the New Testament. This church received the shortest of the seven letters. The word "Smyrna" is based upon "myrrh," an herb that releases a pleasant aroma when crushed. The believers in this city manifested the significance of that name through their sufferings.

9. Read Revelation 2:8, 9. Why would Christ's descriptions of Himself be particularly encouraging to the believers at Smyrna?

Christ described Himself to this church as "the first and the last." He is the God Who controls time and eternity. Through His incarnation Christ conquered death by His own crucifixion and resurrection (Heb. 2:14). Thus, He is also the Lord of death and life (Rev. 2:8). Christ thereby experienced what the Smyrnan believers were anticipating.

In His commendation of the spiritual strength of the church, Christ revealed His awareness of three areas in which they suffered (2:9). First, there was tribulation. Christ had predicted that the world would hate, persecute, ostracize, and kill Christians (John 15:18—16:3, 33). God's children are expected to suffer as well as to believe.

Second, the Smyrnan believers were in severe, abject poverty. They probably had lost their material possessions through persecution and quite possibly had lost their jobs through spiritual oppression. In spite of their financial want, Christ identified them as spiritually wealthy.

Third, the church received opposition (namely blasphemy) from the Jewish element within the city. The unbelieving Jews actually were the instruments of Satan to oppose the work of God.

10. Notice that no complaint is leveled against this church. Why are persecuted churches often pure in their devotion to Christ?

Christ gave one negative and one positive command to Smyrna (2:10). Christ charged the believers not to fear what they were about to suffer. God has not given to His own the spirit of fear; rather, the Holy Spirit produces power, love, and calmness (2 Tim. 1:10). Christ even predicted that Satan would cast some (but not all) into prison. He added that they would have tribulation for ten days. Note the limitation. Believers must allow the test to run its appointed course, but they can be assured that Satan cannot go beyond what God permits.

Christ then commanded them to be faithful unto death. Christ had set the example here (Phil. 2:8). He promised the crown of life to those who endured the test and who loved Him through it.

11. Some people today teach that God will make us healthy,

wealthy, and comfortable if we simply have faith that He will do so. What would the believers at Smyrna say about that notion?

Although believers can be hurt by the first death (the separation of the self from the body), they will never be hurt by the second death, the separation of the unsaved from God in the Lake of Fire (Rev. 2:11). Even physical death cannot divorce the child of God from a loving relationship with God (Rom. 8:35–39).

The Letter to Pergamos

Located north of Smyrna, Pergamos was a wealthy pagan city, especially known for its temples. It contained the temple of Asclepius, the pagan god of medicine, whose idol was in the form of a serpent. The first provincial temple of the imperial cult in Asia (worship of the spirit of Rome and of the emperor, Caesar Augustus) was built there in 29 BC.

Christ is direct in the description of Himself. He is the One Who has "the sharp sword with two edges" (Rev. 2:12). The human responses of belief or disbelief will bring the respective results of either salvation or condemnation (Matt. 7:24–27; John 5:24). His word discriminates between the false and the true (Heb. 4:12).

Pergamos was a morally dark place. It was the dwelling place of Satan, even his throne room (Rev. 2:13). The exaltation of the Roman Caesar as god and the abundance of idolatrous practices supported that analysis. In spite of that hostile environment, the believers were loyal in their allegiance to the deity of Christ. They did not compromise by bowing before the false gods. The believers also maintained an orthodox doctrinal position and practice. Their commendation is noteworthy in that one of their members, Antipas, was martyred for his spiritual steadfastness (2:13). This satanic attack, however, did not weaken their commitment to the Savior.

Christ had two complaints against Pergamos. They tolerated within their membership the presence of some who had compromised their walk (2:14). The reference to Balaam suggests the nature of the trouble that compromise brought.

Balaam (a false prophet in the time of Moses and Joshua) taught Balak (the king of Moab) the method of reducing Israel's effectiveness. Since Israel was in a covenant relationship with God, her position could not be cursed. Balaam thus counseled Balak that if the Israelites were to marry the pagan Moabites and adopt their religious rites and immoral practices (Num. 25:1–3; 31:16), God would become angry with them. Some church members at Pergamos apparently married unsaved pagans, cooperated in idolatrous temple dinners, and even committed immorality.

The church also tolerated those who held the doctrine of the Nicolaitanes. Notice the change from "deeds" (Rev. 2:6) to "doctrine" (2:15).

12. The emerging church movement emphasizes toleration and de-emphasizes doctrine. Why is such an approach harmful to a church?

13. Why might a church think that toleration for sin is admirable?

14. Read Revelation 2:16. Why does God put so much emphasis on His words when writing to the believers at Pergamos (vv. 12, 16)? What do His words have to do with their tolerance and compromise?

The imperative is simple and direct: Repent! The command was actually given to the pastor and to the church. They had the responsibility to discipline the erring members. Failure to take action would bring direct, divine judgment upon the worldly professing believers. The nature of the discipline is not stated. Perhaps premature physical death is implied because, in the historical allusion, Balaam was killed with the sword (Num. 31:8).

Christ gives three promises to the genuine believer/overcomers (Rev. 2:17). First, they would have the satisfying life of Christ, the "hidden manna," which the lost cannot experience. Second, they would have complete justification before God, the Judge of all mankind. The "white stone" was used in ancient legal courts as a sign of acquittal. Third, they would have a new name from God to reflect their change in character. Their inscribed names would demonstrate the value of their position in Christ.

The Letter to Thyatira

Thyatira was a small town about forty miles southeast of Pergamos. It was known for its manufacturing of purple dye and bronze (Acts 16:14). Many pagan trade guilds functioned there. The guilds wielded a lot of power by requiring all those who practiced a trade to be part of the appropriate guild. All members of a guild were required to worship that guild's dieties. Those who refused to worship the deities were barred from practicing their trade. Obviously this was a difficult place for a church to thrive. Being a Christian meant either compromising your faith or losing your job.

15. Read Revelation 2:18. What do the metaphors in this verse reveal about Christ?

Christ emphasized three features about Himself: His title of divine Sonship, His omniscience as seen in the flaming eyes, and His sovereign right of judgment as seen in the feet of brass (Rev. 2:18). These were important attributes for the church at Thyatira to remember as they faced opposition from the powerful guilds.

16. Read Revelation 2:19. What is your first impression of this church?

17. Are you surprised they are described so positively given the challenges they face as citizens of Thyatira? Explain.

Christ commended the church in six areas (v. 19). The church's works were noteworthy. In addition, this is the only church applauded for its love ("charity"). At first look, this church seemed to have it all together.

Christ gave four areas of criticism (v. 20). First, the church gave an evil woman a platform for teaching. Second, the false prophetess spread the false doctrine of conformity to worldly morals and doctrine. What was tolerated in the pew at Pergamos was actually taught in Thyatira. She doubtless encouraged membership and participation in the pagan, idolatrous trade guilds.

Third, an influential group within the church supported this erroneous teaching ("them that commit adultery with her"). Fourth, the union of the false prophetess with her associates produced a generation of false believers ("her children").

18. Are you surprised that some of the church members bought into the woman's message of compromise? Explain. (Question 18)

In His grace and longsuffering, God gave the prophetess and her companions opportunity to repent (2:21–23). Both tribulation and death were to be the consequences for their refusal.

Christ commanded the faithful remnant to "hold fast," implying steadfastness, determination, and integrity (2:24, 25). The reference to the coming of Christ could refer to either the imminent return of the Savior or to His execution of judgment upon the unrepentant crowd.

19. Why is "hold fast" an appropriate exhortation for those in Thyatira who had to choose between serving God and losing their jobs?

The promise in 2:26–29 is different from the others in that it adds the condition of obedience ("and keepeth my works unto the end"). Thus, these promises are given only to the obedient child of God. They involve ruling authority in the millennial Kingdom and full participation in the life of Christ, Who is the morning star. These promises would have been particularly encouraging to those who in Thyatira who were jobless and suffering for the sake of Christ.

Making It Personal

20. Which of Christ's diagnoses have you seen in today's churches?

21. What two or three actions can our church take to assure a positive "diagnosis" from Christ?

22. How are you participating in the work Christ is doing in and through our church?

23. What can you do to prepare yourself to get active in Christ's work through our church?

24. Memorize Revelation 2:4.

Seven Letters to the Churches, Part 2

Christ, as head of the church, discerns, judges, and supports each local church.

Revelation 3

"Behold, I stand at the door, and knock: if any man hear my voice, and open the door, I will come in to him, and will sup with him, and he with me" (Revelation 3:20).

Most people wouldn't appreciate you showing up at their house unannounced and then inviting yourself in once their door is open. That is just plain rude and presumptuous. Yet some people do that repeatedly. Other people don't even knock. They walk right in unannounced. "Surprise! I hope I didn't catch you at a bad time," they sometimes say to soften the fact of their sudden intrusion into your life.

Getting Started

1. Would you ever invite yourself over to someone's house? Explain.

2. Why do most people think it is rude when someone invites himself over to someone else's house?

Christ in a sense has invited Himself over to your life. In fact Revelation 3 describes Him as standing outside a door knocking and waiting to be invited in. You will need to consider whether you have made Christ a welcome guest in your life.

Searching the Scriptures

In the original manuscript of Revelation there were no chapter or verse divisions; thus, there would have been no break between the fourth and fifth letters. Consequently, these seven letters should be studied as a unit.

The Letter to Sardis

Sardis was located thirty miles southeast of Thyatira on the trade route through the region of the ancient kingdom of Lydia. In fact, it served as the capital of that extinct empire. Sardis lost that distinctive glory but still maintained some political prominence under Roman rule in the first century. It became a manufacturing center for textiles, dyes, and jewelry.

Sardis was associated with wealth. The city was one of the earliest minters of coins. The convergence of five roads in the city gave it access to traders while its eight hundred foot cliffs made it easy to defend.

Christ described Himself to Sardis in two ways (Rev. 3:1). First, He has the seven spirits of God. Earlier, the seven spirits were seen before the throne of the Father (1:4). But here, Christ has them. This sevenfold depiction of the Holy Spirit probably refers to Him in His total perfection as the divine enabler for assigned tasks (Isa. 11:2).

Second, Christ has the seven stars, which represent the respective church messengers or pastors. The union of these two descriptions indicates that Christ wanted to direct the work of the earthly witnesses through the enabling of the heavenly Witness. There can be no power apart from the Spirit of God.

3. Has Christ's desire regarding the church changed? Explain.

The only commendation comes in the recognition of a worthy remnant (Rev. 3:4). There were a few godly church members in Smyrna who had not defiled their garments, or yielded to the lusts of the flesh in a worldly environment.

Christ had three complaints against Smyrna. The church had a hypocritical reputation (3:1). It lived a name, but it was dead—impotent and sterile. Christ distinguished between a zealous disciple and a dead, insensitive follower (Luke 9:60).

4. How can a church be dead without even realizing it?

The church was also deteriorating (Rev. 3:2). It was like a patient with a serious illness, but it could be saved. Some dead churches still have some ministries worth salvaging.

The church's imperfect works was the third complaint (3:2). The sense behind "perfect" is that the church failed to bring its goals to completion.

Christ gives the church at Sardis five commands: Be watchful, strengthen, remember, hold fast, and repent (3:2, 3). There still was time for a spiritual recovery; however, the church needed to give it their immediate attention.

5. Read Revelation 3:3. Why would remembering their salvation and past spiritual growth help the Sardis church revive?

Believers must give themselves to prayerful vigilance, or else they will fall to Satan and temptation (1 Pet. 4:7; 5:8). The warning in verse 3 implies that Christ could chastise the church at any moment in unexpected ways.

6. What might a dead church give as excuses for not reviving?

Christ promises Smyrna that the genuine, believing overcomer will be clothed in white raiment (3:5). This refers to the positional garment of imputed righteousness, the wedding robe that gives the believer access to the Marriage Supper of the Lamb (Rev. 19:7–9).

Christ also promised the overcomers that He would not blot their names out of the Book of Life (3:5). Remember that this statement is a promise, not a threat. It is a divine guarantee that the believer will never perish (John 3:16).

Christ's third promise was that He will confess the name of the Christian in Heaven before the Father and the angels (Rev. 3:5).

7. What are you doing to keep your church from becoming a dead church?

8. If everyone put as much effort into the life of your church as you do, would your church have much hope?

The Letter to Philadelphia

The city of Philadelphia was located twenty-eight miles southeast of Sardis. It was situated in a rich agricultural area, but one that was quite earthquake prone. Despite repeated destructive earthquakes, the people did not waver in their purpose to spread Greek culture and language throughout the region. In fact, they were so successful that the city became known as "little Athens."

Christ gave a fourfold description of Himself (3:7). First, He is holy—the personified standard of moral excellence. Second, He is true. He is the epitome of truth, and all that He says and does is in complete conformity with what He is.

9. Why is a belief that God is both true and holy such a key ingredient in persevering as a Christian?

Third, Christ has the key of David. As the Son of David, He is the only One Who can grant admission into the spiritual treasures of the millennial Kingdom. Fourth, He is the One Who opens and shuts doors. He is in sovereign control of human opportunities and activities. He is still in the business of opening doors of ministry today.

10. When have you seen God open a door of opportunity to share the gospel?

Christ doesn't mention a complaint against Philadelphia. The commendation he mentions centers on the concepts of obedience and faithfulness. Christ had presented to the church the open door of witness, and no one could shut it (3:8). Divine power and human integrity are two reasons for this access.

In Philadelphia, the effort to close the gospel witness must have been supported and perhaps led by the synagogue establishment of unsaved Jews (3:9). This group opposed the work at Smyrna also (2:9). The Philadelphian believers were assured that their adversaries would acknowledge the genuine spiritual life of the Christians (3:9).

Christ gives a guarantee to this church in verse 10. Because the believers maintained a living hope in the imminent appearing of Christ, Who could come and deliver them from their persecutions, they were promised total deliverance from the Great Tribulation. The church would not go through that seven-year period itself. This verse supports the position of the pretribulational rapture of the church. The universal trial is designed for earth dwellers (a phrase signifying unbelievers), not for the church saints.

11. Read Revelation 3:11. How would this verse have affected the Philadelphian believers?

Christ gives one charge: hold fast. The object of holding refers to the believers' loving expectation of Christ's return, which had changed the behavior of their lives. The crown refers to the crown of righteousness, which Christ will give to those who live morally pure lives in the light of His imminent coming (2 Tim. 4:8). This concept is joined to Christ's promise, "Behold, I come quickly."

12. How does the imminent return of Christ affect your service for the Lord?

13. Read Revelation 3:12. Why would Christ's promise to make the Philadelphians a "pillar" in God's temple be particularly meaningful to them?

Christ promised the church that He will establish them as pillars in the divine sanctuary. The pillars of pagan temples collapsed when the frequent earthquakes struck, but believers have eternal stability.

Christ stated that the believers have eternal fellowship in the presence of God. Furthermore, Christ will inscribe three names on the child of God. This triple marking shows eternal identification and ownership.

The Letter to Laodicea

Laodicea was located about forty miles southeast of Philadelphia on the road to Colosse. An earthquake destroyed the city in AD 60, but its citizens rebuilt without outside help. That project showed the dominant spirit of self-sufficiency. Paul apparently never visited this city in his missionary travels, but he did communicate with the church there. The name of the city means "judgment of the people."

Christ identified Himself in three ways (3:14). First, He is the "Amen." This term is translated as "verily" in the gospel of John and means "true" or "so be it." Christ's promises can be trusted, and His announcements of judgment will definitely come to pass. Second, He is "the faithful and true witness." He not only is truth, but He speaks the truth. Thus His analysis of the spiritual condition of the church was absolutely correct. Third, He is the originator and ruler of both the natural, created world and the spiritual creation of the church. This statement of creative power identifies Him as the sovereign, eternal God.

This is the only letter that contains no commendation. The lukewarmness of the church was Christ's first complaint (3:15–17). The city received its water supply through an aqueduct system that brought water from hot mineral springs located six miles away. The water naturally cooled down to air temperature by the time it arrived in the city.

14. How do you respond when you drink coffee or tea that has cooled to room temperature?

Spiritual lukewarmness occurs when a Christian allows the pagan attitudes and actions to influence his mind-set and behavior. Just as many people despise lukewarm coffee and water, so Christ declared that He would refuse to tolerate the Laodicean believers in their condition.

15. Read Revelation 3:16. How does Christ respond to lukewarm Christians?

16. What does His reaction tell you about the seriousness of spiritual lukewarmness?

Christ also noted that the church had a faulty evaluation of its spirituality (3:17). Note the contrast between saying and knowing. The assembly saw itself as an affluent, self-sufficient community, but in reality, it was bankrupt. It wrongfully identified financial wealth as a mark of divine favor and personal piety.

Christ gives counsel instead of a direct command (3:18–20). He recommended that the church buy gold, white raiment, and eye salve to correct its spiritual poverty, nakedness, and blindness. Only God can enable a sinner to buy spiritual provisions "without money and without price" (Isa. 55:1, 2).

Genuine believers (described by the phrase "as many as I love") apparently succumbed to the pressure of worldliness and secularism (Rev. 3:19). Christ issued two commands to them: Be zealous and repent. He informed them that He rebukes and chastens His own (cf. Heb. 12:3–15).

17. Read Revelation 3:19. What does God's chastening hand reveal about His relationship with believers?

Christ is knocking on the heart's door of the lukewarm (3:20). He wants to have fellowship with them again. But He waits for them to open the door. They must take the step of returning to fellowship with Christ. They must acknowledge that they need renewed fellowship with Christ.

18. Read Revelation 3:20. If you were a lukewarm believer in Philadelphia, how would you have responded to this verse when you heard it read?

Christ promises the overcomer participation in His earthly reign during the millennial Kingdom (3:21, 22). What a motivation to repent of lukewarmness! Today Christ shares in the Father's sovereign rule over international affairs; in the future, He will rule on earth on the throne of David over a regathered, redeemed Israel.

Making It Personal

19. How does your church reflect some of the problems Christ pointed out in the churches?

20. What prescription might your church need to implement?

21. What part might you have in implementing a prescription for your church?

22. Have you fellowshipped with Christ recently? Is Christ knocking on the door of your heart waiting for you to turn from your sin and invite Him in?

23. What do you need to do in order to restore fellowship with Christ?

24. Memorize Revelation 3:20.

The Throne and the Book

Worship is the believer's natural reaction to God's majesty, character, and power.

Revelation 4; 5

"Saying with a loud voice, Worthy is the Lamb that was slain to receive power, and riches, and wisdom, and strength, and honour, and glory, and blessing" (Revelation 5:12).

Sir Robert Grant was born to privilege. His father, Charles, was a director of the vastly powerful East India Company. Robert himself was no slacker. He served in Parliament, worked for the East India Company, and eventually became governor of Bombay, India. Robert was also a man of faith. One day while reading Psalm 104, Robert responded by writing his own version of the psalm. After Robert's death, his brother published a book of Robert's psalms, including the well-known "O Worship the King."

O Worship the King all glorious above!

O gratefully sing his power and his love,

Our Shield and Defender, the Ancient of days,

Pavilioned in splendor, and girded with praise.

Getting Started

1. What is your favorite worship hymn? Why?

2. What conditions or circumstances prompt worship in you?

This study will focus on a magnificent worship scene in Heaven from which believers can learn much about worship.

Searching the Scriptures

The theme of Revelation 4 and 5 is worship. These chapters also form the introduction to the events that are predicted in the third major section (Rev. 4—22).

Timing of the Rapture

From the premillennial, dispensational viewpoint, all the symbolical and literal actions found in chapters 4—22 have not yet occurred historically. The rapture, or translation, of the church is not described in the book of Revelation. Premillennial evangelicals accept three major views on the time of the Rapture. Both the midtribulational and post-tribulational views contend that the true church, composed of genuine believers, will be on earth during some or all of the events described in the judgment chapters (6—19). The pretribulational position claims that Christ will have taken the true church into Heaven before the events foretold in Revelation 4—22.

For a number of reasons, the content of Revelation best supports the pretribulational view. First, the word "church," so prominently mentioned in the first three chapters, does not appear again until the final chapter (22:16). Second, the church as a corporate body is not seen until the marriage of the Lamb to His wife (19:7). Third, the church has been rewarded in Heaven before Christ actually returns to the earth (19:7–10; cf. 19:11–16). Fourth, the recurring phrase "unto the churches" (2:7, 11, 17, 29; 3:6, 13, 22) is conspicuously absent in a similar admonition (13:9). The reason for this omission is that the church is not on earth to receive it. Fifth, Christ is seen in Heaven in this major section (Rev. 4—19); whereas, earlier He was on earth within the churches. Sixth, if the elders indeed represent the church (4:4; 5:8–10), then the church is already in Heaven before the Great Tribulation begins. Seventh, in the symbolic description of Christ's return to the earth after the Tribulation, there is no mention of the translation of the living redeemed into His presence (19:11–16). If the posttribulational position were correct, then the Rapture should have been declared at this point.

3. How important is the timing of the Rapture to you?

4. How would your outlook on your future be different if you thought you were going to go through the Tribulation?

In chapter 4 the emphasis is on the heavenly throne, God the Father, and the worship of the sovereign, holy God because of His work of creation. In the next chapter, the stress is on the seven-sealed scroll, Jesus Christ, and the worship of the Savior because of His work of redemption.

The Summons

5. Read Revelation 4:1. Put yourself in John's place. How do you think you would respond to a call to enter Heaven to see future events?

After writing down "the things which are" (indicated by the phrases "after this" and "hereafter"), John looked up and beheld an open door in Heaven. The apostle entered this door and thus saw the future from God's perspective.

The Father and the Throne

Upon his entrance into Heaven, John first saw a throne. The verb form in verse 2 indicates that the throne was being placed into position (literally "was being set up") for a special purpose. The content of the following chapters shows that this throne relates to the redemption of Israel and the destruction of Israel's enemies.

The occupant of the throne is God the Father. The two precious stones, jasper and sardine (sardonyx), reveal God's faithfulness as the sovereign Protector of Israel (4:3). These two stones were found with ten others on the breastplate of the Jewish high priest (Ex. 28:17–21). The twelve stones represented the twelve tribes of Israel. The first stone was the sardine ("sardius"), the stone for the tribe of Reuben, the oldest of the twelve sons. The last stone was the jasper for the tribe of Benjamin, the youngest of the twelve sons. In Revelation 4:3, therefore, God is seen in His covenant relationship with Israel, faithful to His pledged word: "I will bless them that bless thee, and curse him that curseth thee" (Gen. 12:3).

6. At that time, what were the circumstances on earth regarding Israel?

7. What would John have learned about God when he saw the stones that represented Israel, God's covenant people?

The emerald green rainbow (Rev. 4:3) further reinforces the concept of divine promise and faithfulness. The future survival of Israel rests upon neither her military strength nor her alliances with the West; only God can deliver her from the terrors of the Great Tribulation.

The Twenty-four Elders

John then saw twenty-four seats (literally "thrones") in a circle around the throne of God (4:4). On the miniature thrones were twenty-four elders. The elders most likely represent redeemed people since the clothing of white raiment suggests the imputed righteousness of Christ, and the crowns of gold points to the rewards of spiritual victory.

8. Why is the presence of the twenty-four elders a reminder of God's grace?

The elders represent only the redeemed of the Church Age in a royal priestly function rather than Israel and the church. During his reign, King David divided the Levitical priesthood into twenty-four orders. Each order, when it functioned, represented the entire priesthood and the nation of Israel (1 Chron. 24). All believers today are constituted a royal priesthood (1 Pet. 2:9; Rev. 1:6). Thus, the elders in Heaven show that the church has already been translated and rewarded before the Great Tribulation begins.

The Four Living Creatures

John then observed four "living ones" or "living beings" (literal translation), probably angels (4:6). The beings are extremely alert and sensitive. Note that they are "full of eyes before and behind" (v. 8). The possession of six wings probably indicates that they are ready and quick to obey the divine commands. They are constantly praising God for His holiness, sovereignty, and eternal existence.

9. Read Revelation 4:8. Why wouldn't the four living creatures rest day or night? What does their constant praising of God tell you about the praiseworthiness of God?

There is much speculation about the four designations of lion, calf, man, and eagle (v. 7). In the wilderness wanderings of Israel, the twelve tribes encamped about the tabernacle in four groups of three tribes each. Each group had a tribal leader. According to tradition, the standards for the four leaders were these: Judah, lion; Ephraim, ox; Reuben, man; and Dan, eagle. The four creatures thus may represent God's sovereign control over the nation of Israel.

10. What are some reasons for worshiping God based on Revelation 4?

The Book Viewed by John

11. Read Revelation 5:1–4. Why did John begin to weep?

12. Why did John want the book to be opened?

The scroll in the hand of the Father is actually a scroll written on both sides. It is also sealed with seven seals. What is the significance of this book? The sealed scroll in God's hand is the title deed to planet Earth.

God gave to Adam and to mankind the right of earthly dominion, but man lost that right through his sin (Gen. 1:26; Heb. 2:5–8). The second Adam, Jesus Christ, became Man and died on the cross to regain for man, namely in Himself, that lost dominion (Heb. 2:9). Christ will claim what is rightfully His through the series of judgments revealed in the opening of the seven seals.

After seeing the book, John saw a mighty angel (Rev. 5:2). This angel asked a probing question: "Who is worthy to open the book, and to loose the seals thereof?" The issue in question is the person's innate, moral worth. The response comes back that no one in Heaven or earth—no angel or human being—is worthy (5:3). John began to weep out of spiritual despair because no one was found worthy (5:4).

13. Why would not finding anyone worthy to open the scroll be so disastrous?

The Book Taken by Christ

One of the elders then told John to stop weeping (5:5). He informed the apostle that there was One Who was worthy and Who had prevailed to open the book. The elder then identified Christ in two ways. First, He is the Lion of the tribe of Judah. When the patriarch Jacob was on his deathbed, he gave a series of predictions concerning his twelve sons. He identified Judah as the one through whom the promised Messiah would come: "Judah, thou art he whom thy brethren shall praise. . . . Judah is a lion's whelp" (Gen. 49:8–10).

Second, He is also the root of David (Rev. 5:5). David began a dynasty of kings who ruled over Judah for four hundred years. In 586 BC the Babylonians conquered the Jewish kingdom and ended the line of Davidic rulers. For about six hundred years, Davidic rule appeared to be dead as various Gentile powers occupied Jerusalem. In the fullness of time, however, a live root, or shoot, sprang out of Israel's spiritual deadness. Christ became the One in Whom all of the royal promises will be fulfilled (2 Sam. 7:12–16; Luke 1:30–33).

John then saw a symbolic vision of Christ in the midst of the throne, the elders, and the four living creatures (Rev. 5:6). First, he saw a young lamb. Christ, of course, died at an early age. Second, the fact that the lamb had been slain is a reference to the crucifixion. Third, the slain lamb stood, an indication of resurrection. Fourth, the seven horns seem to refer to the prerogatives of total kingship and strength over the seven continents of planet Earth (Dan. 7:24). Fifth, the possession of the seven spirits shows that He is the Anointed One (Rev. 5:6).

The Songs of Rejoicing

When Christ took the scroll, three anthems of sincere praise sounded forth. There was no pretense in these anthems.

14. Read Revelation 5:8–14. What reasons for worshiping Christ are included in the anthems?

The first anthem was by the twenty-four elders (5:8–10). Both the four living creatures and the elders prostrated themselves before Christ, but the grammar of the verse indicates that only the elders had the harps and vials and sang the song. The odors within the vials are identified as the prayers of saints (cf. Ps. 141:2). They doubtless include prayers for the vindication of God's name, for judgment upon wicked men, and for the establishment of the Kingdom of God (Matt. 6:10). In their song, the elders ascribe worth to Christ for His crucifixion, His redemption of them, and His appointment of them to be kings and priests (Rev. 5:9, 10). The elders then express their confidence that they will reign on earth with Christ (cf. Matt. 19:28; 2 Tim. 2:12).

15. How does the scene in Revelation 5:8–10 help you understand the necessity of Christ's death for our redemption?

16. How does this scene affect the praise of gratitude you have for the Lord?

The second outburst of rejoicing comes from innumerable angels (Rev. 5:11, 12). They mention that Christ is worthy to receive seven things of greatest value because of His death.

The third song of praise involves the entire creation (5:13, 14). In addition to redeemed mankind and the holy angels, this group could include the created world of birds, animals, and fish (cf. Rom. 8:19–22). The value of Christ's death extends to the removal of the curse upon the animal and vegetable kingdoms.

17. Read Revelation 5:14. What besides worshiping the Lord could be more thrilling when we get to Heaven?

Making It Personal

18. What made the heavenly worship scene in Revelation 4 and 5 so sincere?

19. How can you make sure your worship is sincere?

20. What worship ideas, drawn from today's study, can help you in your personal worship throughout this week?

21. What do you need to do in order to incorporate worship of God into your daily life?

22. What might be some ways to remind yourself to worship God throughout the day?

23. Memorize Revelation 5:12.

The Seal Judgments

*Christ, as the Lamb, is the judge of the ungodly
but the Savior of the redeemed.*

Revelation 6; 7

**"For the Lamb which is in the midst of the throne
shall feed them, and shall lead them unto living
fountains of waters: and God shall wipe away
all tears from their eyes" (Revelation 7:17).**

Judges have one of the stateliest and most serious jobs. For that reason a farmer probably wouldn't ask a judge to help him herd his cows or slop his hogs. No one would expect a judge to be a shepherd of sheep either. The judge's bailiff wouldn't get much of a response from the sheep if he asked them to "all rise" when the judge entered the pasture.

Getting Started

1. What are some characteristics of a judge? What are some traits of a shepherd?

2. What would you think of someone who was both a judge and a shepherd?

Revelation presents Christ's dual roles as both a judge and a shepherd during the Tribulation. Both roles reveal His character, which is without fault. Both roles also help us understand Christ and our relationship with Him.

Searching the Scriptures

We now come to the major section of the book, the judgment chapters (6:1—19:10). These chapters contain three series of seven judgments each: seven seals (6:1—8:1), seven trumpets (8:2—11:19), and seven vials or bowls (15:1—16:21).

The first six seals are discussed in Revelation 6, but the seventh seal is mentioned later (8:1) after a parenthesis is inserted (Rev. 7). The Lamb, Jesus Christ, opens the seals because only He has the right and power to do so as the possessor of the title deed, or scroll. After each of the first four seals is opened, one of the four living creatures issues a command: "Come and see." This charge is naturally directed toward John.

First Seal

3. Read Revelation 6:1. How does the thunderous voice help to set the tone for the events that are about to unfold?

The voice of the first living creature sounds like thunder. This thunder at the outset of the Great Tribulation heralds the ominous divine judgments and human atrocities.

The white horse and its rider symbolize the Antichrist. Technically, the great tribulation period begins when the Antichrist makes a seven-year covenant with the nation of Israel (Dan. 9:24–27).

The Antichrist pledges to protect Israel against outside attack if Israel agrees to surrender occupied territory and to begin disarmament. Israel thus sees in the rider a political savior. The white color shows that he is a counterfeit messiah, because Christ Himself will return to the earth on a white horse after the Tribulation (19:11).

4. What is indicated by the fact that the rider on the white horse has a bow but no arrows?

Daniel predicted that the false messiah would destroy many by means of peaceful negotiations (Dan. 8:25). Paul declared that destruction would swiftly follow the cries of peace in the Day of the Lord (1 Thess. 5:3).

Satan gave this rider, the Antichrist, a crown (Rev. 6:2). The false messiah will gladly accept this satanic gift (13:2). His ultimate goal is to conquer the entire world.

5. What circumstances in the world would seem to be laying the foundation for the Antichrist to gain world domination in the Tribulation?

Second Seal

The second horse is red, the color of blood and the indelible mark of warfare (6:3). John saw that this rider had power to take peace from the earth.

Ezekiel predicted that in the latter times of Israel's future, there would be an invasion of the land from the north (Ezek. 38:8ff). This northern invader, probably Russia, will come when the nation of Israel is at rest and unprepared for war (38:11).

Modern Israel has built its military, called the Israel Defense Force (IDF), into one of the world's strongest. Something must happen that will cause Israel to surrender her weapons. That event must be the covenant of protection with the false messiah. Russia thus takes advantage of Israel's weakness and moves toward the Promised Land. The results will be the removal of peace, great killing, and awesome bloodshed.

Third Seal

6. Read Revelation 6:5, 6. What two words would you use to describe life on earth at this point of the Tribulation?

7. How would imagining lost neighbors and family members scavenging for food help create a desire in you to witness to them?

The black horse represents suffering from hunger. The balances show that food will be such a precious commodity that it will be weighed carefully (6:5). It will take a day's wage to purchase a measure of wheat to provide one adequate meal for one person. The three measures of barley will be ample for three persons to have one meal each, but the food content will be less nutritious. Oil and wine—used as medicine, in cooking, or as a beverage—will be extremely costly items.

Fourth Seal

8. Read Revelation 6:7, 8. How do these verses affect you as you read them?

The fourth horse is pale, a yellowish-green. The rider is Death, and its companion is Hell, or Hades. At death, all unsaved go into these two realms—death for the body and Hell for the spirit.

Four means are used to achieve the judgment of this seal: the sword, referring to international warfare and internal rioting; hunger from famine; death, probably a reference to pestilence including disease, toxic wastes, and chemical/biological weapons; and wild animals.

The scope of the judgment affects one-fourth of the earth, most likely a reference to the total population of the earth.

Fifth Seal

9. Read Revelation 6:9–11. What will life be like for people who trust Christ during the Tribulation?

With the opening of the fifth seal, the scene changes from earth to Heaven. John saw believers who had been martyred during the events of the first four seals. The martyrs cry out for divine vengeance upon their earthly adversaries. The answer to their prayer is that judgment will come, but only after more believers are killed (6:11).

Sixth Seal

The scene now changes from Heaven to earth (6:12). The sixth seal actually contains six events. First, there is a great earthquake. Christ predicted that earthquakes would be one of the signs of the Great Tribulation (Matt. 24:7).

10. Read Revelation 6:12. What problems does a devastating earthquake cause?

The second and third events are the blackening of the sun and the reddening of the moon (Rev. 6:12). Again, Jesus prophesied the presence of heavenly signs (Luke 21:11, 25). These phenomena will decrease both heat and light and will compound the problems left by the massive earthquake.

The fourth event is a shower of huge meteorites that penetrates the earth's atmosphere and impacts the planet's surface (Rev. 6:13). The fifth event of this seal reveals a convulsion of the planets and stars (6:14). The sixth event is the collapse and disappearance of mountains and islands caused by the earthquake and mammoth tidal waves.

11. Read Revelation 6:15–17. What good will money and power be to people on earth during this time?

12. What do the people on earth recognize about the source of the widespread devastation?

Instead of repenting, the unsaved seek refuge in the caverns of the earth from this display of divine wrath (6:15). They attribute the six events to God, not to international warfare (vv. 16, 17).

God makes it clear through the events of the sixth seal that His wrath is directing the devastation on earth. As the judge of the earth He is quite frightening. Both small and great will fear Him and seek to escape His wrath.

Delay of Judgment

Revelation 7 contains a parenthetical insertion of vital content between the sixth seal (6:12–17) and the opening of the seventh seal (8:1). It contains three basic features.

John saw four angels holding, or restraining, the four winds of the earth: the north wind, the south wind, the east wind, and the west wind. The Bible employs the language of appearance and communication when it refers to scientific matters. The earth neither is flat nor has four corners.

A fifth angel charged the four angels not to release their winds until the servants of God had been sealed in their foreheads. God is sovereign; thus He can control and use the phenomena of winds to destroy the earth and the sea.

The 144,000

The servants of God, sealed in their foreheads, are now identified (7:4–8). They consist of 12,000 Jews from each of the twelve tribes of Israel. These 144,000 Jewish servants apparently are saved during the events of the first six seal judgments through the illumination of the Holy Spirit. Christ announced that the gospel of the Kingdom would be proclaimed in the Great Tribulation (Matt. 24:14). That message would be "Repent, for the kingdom of heaven is at hand!" Why? Because the King, even Jesus Christ, is coming soon to earth. Since all genuine living believers of the Church Age are translated into Heaven before the advent of the Great Tribulation, God must save these Jewish servants after the Rapture. There is no indication as to the nature of their service, but they could be preachers and witnesses.

13. What do you learn about God through His provision of a strong witness during the Tribulation?

The Great Multitude

14. Read Revelation 7:9–14. What is the connection between God's wrath and the great multitude of tribulation believers in Heaven?

John then saw an innumerable host in Heaven (7:9). They came from all of the nations of the earth. They thus are Gentiles mainly, but the number could also include the Jewish people. These are redeemed people. They are clothed with the robes of imputed divine righteousness made white by the cleansing of Christ's blood. In their hands they hold palms, the symbol of rejoicing for divinely imparted salvation.

Their lips testify to the fact that they are saved (7:10–12). They are joined by the angels in their worship and adoration.

This great number of converts "are the ones who are coming out of the Tribulation, the great one" (7:14; literal translation). This description indicates that these are believers who are saved and martyred during the Great Tribulation. Verses 15–17 name ten provisions of divine blessing that will be theirs in Heaven after their suffering on earth.

15. Read Revelation 7:15–17. What will the tribulation saints want to do once they are in God's presence in Heaven?

16. What will the Lamb do for the tribulation believers?

17. What do we learn about Christ through seeing Him as the Lamb of God shepherding the tribulation believers?

The remarkable paradox indicated by this scene is that the Tribulation will not only be the period of the greatest divine judgments poured out upon the earth, but it will also be the time of the greatest harvest of souls and the era of the most severe persecution of believers. All of these developments occur within the space of seven years.

Making It Personal

We all deserve not only to experience the troubles of the Tribulation but also to spend eternity in the Lake of Fire. God has saved us from His wrath through Christ.

18. How should you respond when you realize that you stand before God your Judge as cleansed from your sins?

19. Write a praise to God for salvation and for escaping His wrath.

20. As a believer Christ shepherds you and cares for you. How should you respond to Christ, Who will shepherd you forever?

21. Write a praise to God for His loving care.

22. Memorize Revelation 7:17.

The Trumpet Judgments

God's judgments are certain, severe, and appropriate for righteousness to be vindicated.

Revelation 8—10

"But the LORD shall endure for ever: he hath prepared his throne for judgment. And he shall judge the world in righteousness, he shall minister judgment to the people in uprightness" (Psalm 9:7, 8).

Some people doubt God's goodness or even His existence by pointing to all the tragedies, disasters, and diseases in the world. How could God be good if He allows so many problems in the world? Those people obviously have never read Revelation, a book filled with accounts of God's direct judgment on humanity. The list is not pretty.

What critics of the Bible would not understand is that humanity will deserve every judgment God gives to them. And the judgments come hard and often because the lost will refuse to repent.

Getting Started

1. List common characteristics of a person who refuses to repent of his or her wrong.

2. When have you seen someone refuse to repent even in the face of terrible consequences for their actions?

God's trumpet judgments on the earth during the Tribulation are severe, yet many people don't repent of their sins. This lesson will examine the trumpet judgments and the fact that God remains righteous through them all.

Searching the Scriptures

The first six seals are described in Revelation 6. The parenthesis, or interlude, between the sixth and seventh seals introduces us to the 144,000 Jewish servants and the innumerable host of Gentile converts (7:1–17).

Seventh Seal

When Christ opens the seventh seal, a great silence hushes Heaven for thirty minutes (8:1). The rejoicing of the tribulation saints stops (7:9–17).

3. Read Revelation 8:1. What might the complete silence have communicated to those in God's presence in Heaven?

The scene moves to the introduction of the seven angels with the seven trumpet judgments. This fact shows that the seven trumpet judgments are contained within the seventh seal and actually explain the content of the seventh seal.

An eighth angel then appears at the heavenly altar. In his censer is incense, which he offers with the prayers of the saints (8:3, 4; cf. 5:8). The significance of this action is that both holy angels and redeemed humans want God to judge the world of wicked angels and people (6:10) and to usher in the Kingdom of everlasting righteousness.

4. Read Revelation 8:3. Why is praying for God's judgment to come appropriate?

The angel then fills the censer with the fire of the altar and casts it toward the earth (8:5). This action is accompanied by four signs that indicate imminent divine judgment. It also provides a signal for the seven angels to blow their trumpets in planned sequence (8:6). The prayers of the redeemed are about to be answered.

5. Read Revelation 8:4, 5. How should this scene affect how seriously you take your prayers?

First Trumpet

The first trumpet judgment contains the phenomena of hail and fire mingled with blood (8:7). This judgment is similar to the seventh plague of God upon the Egyptians in the time of Moses (Exod. 9:18–35). God directly intervened in the affairs of Egypt and Israel with a sovereign use of thunderstorms and lightning. Although vegetation is the main target of the first trumpet, the mention of blood indicates that human and animal life will also be affected.

The destruction by fire of one-third of the trees and the green grass on the earth will deal a devastating blow to the ecology of the land and its ability to sustain both animal and vegetable food.

6. What does the first trumpet judgment communicate about God and His power?

Second Trumpet

This second judgment will affect the saltwater oceans (Rev. 8:8). John saw what appeared as a mountain burning with fire descend into the sea. The qualifying words ("as it were") show that it was not a real mountain. John could have seen a mammoth meteorite plunging through the atmosphere in a fiery path toward the sea. Meteors have impacted the earth occasionally, but most are consumed early in their entry into the atmosphere that surrounds the planet. Of course God is not limited by what seems plausible or natural.

The result of the impact is that the sea becomes blood. God causes the water to become blood. In one of the famous plagues upon the Egyptians, God changed the waters of the Nile and its tributaries into actual blood (Exod. 7:19–21).

One-third of the sea creatures will perish in this second trumpet judgment. This group includes both fish and water mammals. Human life will also be lost because one-third of the ships will be destroyed through the direct hit and subsequent tidal wave.

Third Trumpet

When the third angel sounded his trumpet, John saw a great star burning like an ancient lamp and falling toward the freshwater systems (Rev. 8:10). It specifically fell upon the third part of the rivers. "Fountains of water" refers to the mountainous sources of the freshwater rivers and could possibly allude to mountain lakes or reservoirs.

In Revelation 8:11, the name of the star is Wormwood, from a bitter plant that grows in desert places. In their thirst, human beings will drink the poisonous waters caused by this star, and they will die.

7. What do the second and third trumpet judgments communicate about God and His power?

Fourth Trumpet

The fourth trumpet judgment focuses on heavenly signs (8:12). One-third of the sun, moon, and stars are smitten. This action is further explained by the facts that one-third of them are darkened, that the day did not shine for one-third of its twelve-hour cycle, and that the night did not shine for its twelve-hour cycle from dusk to dawn.

These phenomena have plausible explanations. First, the length of the normal calendar day (twenty-four hours) may be reduced to sixteen hours. Second, there may be a decrease in the output of light and heat by these heavenly bodies to the extent of one-third.

8. What does the fourth trumpet judgment communicate about God and His power?

John then saw and heard an angel flying through the midst of Heaven (8:13). The angel declared that the final three trumpet judgments would be worse than the first four. To emphasize this fact, the angel named the fifth, sixth, and seventh trumpets as the three woes. The judgments would basically fall upon the inhabitants of the earth, a term synonymous with the unsaved during the tribulation period.

Fifth Trumpet

When the fifth angel sounded his trumpet, John saw a fallen star (9:1). Who or what is this star? There are three possibilities. It could refer to a meteorite or to a modern weapon that opens the earth upon its impact. It could refer to a good angel. Personal pronouns (he, him) are ascribed to the star (9:2), and the activity of opening is a work of a person, not of an inanimate object. Later, a good angel has the key of the abyss and binds Satan within it (20:1–3). Or, it could refer to an evil angel, quite possibly to Satan.

The star opens the bottomless pit, literally, "the shaft of the abyss." Out of the abyss comes a dark smoke, similar to that which a furnace produces. It is both thick and vast enough to blacken the sun and the air. Out of the smoke come locusts (9:3).

Who or what are the locusts? Some regard them as modern weapons, such as helicopters or bombers. They could also be symbolic of demons. Or, they might be literal insects. The description seems to indicate symbolism (9:7–10).

These creatures obey commands; thus they appear to be personal beings with the attribute of volition (9:4). However, they are charged not to attack vegetation, normally an object of insect devastation. They attack human beings and actually discriminate between the redeemed and the unsaved, afflicting only the latter. They inflict pain similar to that of a scorpion's sting (9:5, 10). They torment men for five months, the normal period of a locust plague. Swarms of locusts do not have leaders (Prov. 30:27), but this band has a king (Rev. 9:11).

9. Read Revelation 9:6. How do the unsaved react to the stinging locusts?

10. What do those still alive on earth learn about God through the fifth trumpet?

Sixth Trumpet

The sixth trumpet judgment contains elements just as bizarre as the fifth. John first heard a voice coming from the golden altar (9:13). Since the altar is situated before God, the voice probably belongs to that of the eighth angel who stands at the altar (8:3). The voice issues a command to the sixth trumpet angel: "Loose the four angels which are bound in the great river Euphrates" (9:14). Scripture does not indicate that holy angels are ever bound; therefore, these must be evil angels, bound and prepared for a special work in the Tribulation. The Euphrates River is a natural water boundary between the Middle East and the

Far East. The land area promised to Abraham extends on the east to the Euphrates.

The loosed angels have one purpose—to kill the third part of men (9:15). In the fourth seal, one-fourth of mankind is destroyed (6:8). In the sixth trumpet judgment one-third of the remaining three-fourths will die. If this terminology is universal in scope, then one-half of the earth's population will be decimated at the conclusion of the sixth trumpet. This destruction will happen in a limited time period (9:15).

The means of killing by the four angels will be an army of 200 million (9:16). This could be an army of evil angels or wicked men, probably the latter. Some have identified this massive army as the movement of the kings of the east toward the Promised Land (16:12). This group would thus include Red China and her Asian allies. The loss of human life would occur on the land bridge between China and Israel, embracing such countries as Iran, Pakistan, India, Bangladesh, and Burma.

The weapons are described as fire, smoke, and brimstone (9:17, 18), perhaps a reference to some sort of nuclear weapons.

11. Read Revelation 9:20, 21. What don't the unsaved do as a result of the trumpet judgments?

12. What would the unsaved expect their idols and the gods they represent to do for them?

13. What do we learn about the depth of the depravity of man from these verses?

The result of this bloodshed is that the living refuse to repent of their sins (9:20, 21). This statement shows that the brunt of these judgments falls upon the unsaved.

Book Held by the Angel

Before the seventh angel sounds his trumpet, there is a parenthesis or interlude (10:1—11:14).

Some commentators have identified the angel in Revelation 10:1 as Christ, but this angel is most likely another mighty angel. Angels often appear in a brilliance similar to that belonging to God (cf. 28:2, 3). The angel in Revelation 10 holds a little book (10:2); whereas Christ possesses a regular book (5:6-8).

The angel declares that the mystery of God will be finished during the scope of the seventh trumpet (10:7). The mystery involves the total completion of God's prophetic program for Israel, revealed in Daniel's prophecy of seventy weeks (Dan. 9:24–27; Rom. 11:25). The program of the church ("the things which are"; 1:19) is an insertion into the program for Israel between the sixty-ninth and seventieth weeks. After the rapture of the church, God will begin the period of the seventieth week, namely the Great Tribulation.

14. Read Revelation 10:7. Will God's judgments and plans ever be stopped according to this verse?

Book Eaten by John

Following instructions, John took the book from the angel and ate it (10:8, 9). It was sweet in his mouth but bitter in his stomach (10:10). Revelation from God is wonderful to receive, but the blessing of the establishment of the theocratic Kingdom upon the earth can be achieved only by the destruction of the unsaved.

15. What do you find most difficult about studying God's Tribulation judgments?

16. What do you find sweet as you study the coming blessings of eternal life with God?

Making It Personal

17. Keeping this study of God's trumpet judgments in mind, how certain and severe are God's judgments?

18. Why are God's judgments appropriate?

19. How should you respond to the trumpet judgments?

20. What can you do or say to "trumpet" to the lost their desperate need for salvation?

21. Memorize Psalm 9:7 and 8.

Lesson 7

The Holy Conflicts

Praise to God is sharpened by a contrast between good and evil.

Revelation 11; 12

"We give thee thanks, O Lord God Almighty, which art, and wast, and art to come; because thou hast taken to thee thy great power, and hast reigned" (Revelation 11:17).

Rain, crickets, mosquitoes, poison ivy, sleeping bags, tents, and open-air bathrooms are all part of the roughing it experience. At the onset of a camping trip, those things don't seem like a big deal. But by the end of the trip they become a huge deal. When the campers finally return home things like a shower, a refrigerator, a recliner, a bed, and four walls and a roof seem like heaven. Camping brings an appreciation for what we often take for granted.

Getting Started

1. List some things that are better observed when seen in contrast with something else.

2. Why does the contrast between good and evil sharpen praise to God?

Searching the Scriptures

The major features of Revelation 11 and 12 fit into the literary scheme of the book as two parentheses (interludes) before and after the seventh trumpet judgment. The measuring of the temple and the account of the two witnesses conclude the parenthesis between the sixth and seventh trumpets. The seventh trumpet is then described (11:15–19). Afterward, a lengthy parenthesis—including the holy war—is inserted before the bowl (or vial) judgments are set forth in Revelation 15 and 16.

Measuring the Temple

An angel gave John a straight measuring reed, probably about ten feet long (11:1). The angel then charged John to become a participant in the prophetic vision. He commanded the apostle to measure three items within the temple area, which will be in use by the middle of the Tribulation (11:1). This measurement was likely a kind of survey of God's possession.

The temple spoken of here actually refers to the inner temple sanctuary, with both the holy place and the Holy of Holies. The altar is probably the altar of sacrifice. We know that animal sacrifices will be offered in the Tribulation temple because the Antichrist will later force them to be stopped (Dan. 9:27). The worshipers of Revelation 11:1 are doubtless the ritualistic Jews of that period.

The angel charged John not to measure the court of the Gentiles (11:2), the large open area to the south of the sanctuary building. This measurement is prohibited because Gentiles would again control the temple area and the holy city of Jerusalem for forty-two months, namely the last three and a half years of the Tribulation.

Ministry of the Two Witnesses

3. Name some witnesses that proclaimed God's messages during dark times of rampant apostasy.

Several features of the witnesses' character and work are recorded in Revelation 11. First they are energized by God (11:3). They are divinely regenerated, gifted, and empowered. Second, they prophesy for 1,260 days (forty-two months or three and one-half years). There is debate as to whether they minister in the first half or the second half of the Tribulation. It is difficult to say with certainty. Third, their garments show that they are mourning over the disobedience of the Jewish nation. They are prophets of doom, lamenting the imminent judgment of God upon His covenant people.

4. How popular would you expect the two witnesses to be as they proclaimed God's message of doom?

Fourth, the two witnesses are divine representatives (11:4). They are likened to olive trees and to candlesticks. They thus are fruit and light-bearers before God.

5. Read Revelation 11:4 and John 3:19, 20. Why are godly believers often hated by the lost?

6. When have you been in a situation where your godliness shone as a light against the lives of the lost around you?

7. How did you react to such a situation?

Fifth, the two witnesses are divinely protected from their enemies (Rev. 11:5). If any opponent wills to hurt them, the witnesses will merely speak, and the enemy will be destroyed. Sixth, they have delegated power to perform miracles (11:6). Like Elijah, they will be able to keep it from raining for three and one-half years. Like Moses, they will be able to change water into blood and to smite the earth with plagues.

8. What message about sin is God giving through His two witnesses?

Seventh, their identity is unknown. Most commentators see them as Moses and Elijah but there is no way to know for sure.

Martyrdom of the Two Witnesses

After the two witnesses finish their testimony for God, they will be martyred (Rev. 11:7). These men will seal the proclamation of their lips with the sacrifice of their lives. With God's sovereign permission, their enemy will kill them.

Their adversary is the beast that ascends out of the bottomless pit, the abyss. This symbolic title represents a real person, namely the Antichrist. By this action, the false messiah will eliminate his two divinely sanctioned opponents and will reveal himself to be what he truly is. At this time, he will also break his seven-year covenant with Israel (Dan. 9:24–27).

The bodies of the two witnesses are put on public display in the city of Jerusalem (Rev. 11:8). Representatives from all of the nations then view the bodies (11:9). The authorities will not permit the bodies to be buried during this period of three and one-half days.

9. Read Revelation 11:10. How do the unsaved respond to the death of the two witnesses?

10. Why might the unsaved respond in that manner? What might they think has "died" along with the witnesses?

Resurrection of the Two Witnesses

11. Read Revelation 11:11, 12. What is God communicating to the lost by resurrecting the witnesses and taking them to Heaven?

God interrupts the brief celebration, however, and resurrects the two witnesses after the period of three and one-half days (11:11). Divinely energized, the two stand to their feet to the amazement of the unsaved onlookers. God immediately calls them into Heaven, and they ascend bodily in the sight of their enemies (11:12).

12. How do those who see the resurrections and ascensions respond (v. 12)?

Just as an earthquake accompanied the death and resurrection of Jesus Christ, so now there is an earthquake that levels one-tenth of Jerusalem, causing the death of seven thousand men (11:13). These miraculous phenomena cause the survivors in the city to be afraid and give glory to God (cf. 12:17).

The parenthesis, with its description of the angel, the book, the measurement of the temple sanctuary, and the ministry of the two witnesses is now over. It thus brings to a close the second woe, the sixth trumpet (11:14).

The Seventh Trumpet

The sounding of the seventh trumpet introduces the third woe (11:15, cf. 8:13). Within the time scheme of the Tribulation, it seems to occur at the middle of the period and actually lasts to the very end. In other words, the events that take place during the sounding of the seventh trumpet will happen during the last three and one-half years.

Verses 15 to 19 summarize the key events of the seventh trumpet. For one thing, the transfer of the kingdoms of this world to God and to Christ will take place (11:15). Although the Antichrist will rule as an absolute dictator, he will meet his end at Armageddon (16:13–16; 19:17–21). After destroying the wicked nations, Christ will then establish His eternal Kingdom. The elders respond in worship and vocal praise to God for asserting His divine right to rule over the affairs of men (11:16, 17).

13. Read Revelation 11:17, 18. For what do the twenty-four elders praise God?

The nations of the earth will be angry because they know they will receive the wrath of God in the remaining three and one-half years (11:18). God's wrath will be fully described in the outpouring of the seven bowl judgments (15:1, 7; 16:1, 17).

The dead will be raised and judged at the return of Christ to the earth (11:18; 20:4–6). This resurrection will include the redeemed of the Tribulation who have died and probably the saints of the Old Testament era (Dan. 12:1–3). This event will complete the prophetic program for the nation of Israel (Dan. 9:24–27).

The temple of God was opened in Heaven, and John saw the ark of the covenant (Rev. 11:19). This vision confirms that God will support His covenant relationship with Israel.

14. Read Revelation 11:19. The church is not part of God's covenant relationship with Israel, so why should believers care if God keeps His covenant with Israel?

The five phenomena listed in verse 19 are indicators of imminent divine judgment upon the enemies of Israel. This vision, delayed by a lengthy parenthesis (12:1—14:20), will resume when the seven angels with the seven bowl judgments will come out of the heavenly temple (15:1—16:21).

The spiritually sensitive are aware that an unseen war between God and Satan has been going on since Creation. Often they are able to see the visible expression of this war in actual history. This holy war will reach its climax during the last half of the Tribulation.

The Woman

John then saw a great wonder, or sign, in Heaven. A Biblical sign is an object or event with spiritual significance.

The woman in the sign represents the nation of Israel as the channel through which the Messiah-Redeemer will come (12:1). The sun refers to Jacob, whose name was changed to Israel; the moon, to Leah; and the twelve stars, to the twelve tribes of Israel. One of Joseph's dreams is the basis of this interpretation (Gen. 37:9, 10). The original Messianic promise stated that God would destroy Satan through the seed of the woman (Gen. 3:15). From Eve to Sarah, the line centered in the pre-Hebrew genealogical line, but from Sarah to Mary the line was carried on through the nation of Israel.

The Dragon

Satan is seen as the great red dragon (12:3), symbolic of his power, ferocity, and murderous character (John 8:44). The seven crowned heads and ten horns identify him as the supernatural force behind the kingdom of the Antichrist. The seven heads probably represent the seven major nations that Satan has used to oppress the Jewish people and the final empire led by the Antichrist. The ten horns are the ten-nation confederation that forms the nucleus of the kingdom of the Antichrist.

The heavenly stars cast to earth (Rev. 12:4) seem to be angels who followed Lucifer in his rebellion against God (Isa. 14:12–17); thus Satan is the leader of one-third of the divinely created angels.

Ever since the prediction that he would be destroyed by the Seed of the woman, Satan has conspired to kill one link of the Messianic line to prevent the divine-human Redeemer from coming into the world.

15. Read Revelation 12:4. When has Satan tried to destroy either the royal line or Christ Himself?

16. What might the future hold if Satan had triumphed over Christ? (This was never a possibility, though.)

17. When was the last time you praised God for His sovereign control of history and subsequent provision of salvation?

The Child

The man-child is definitely Jesus Christ (12:5). The symbolic sign quickly moves from Christ's birth to His bodily ascension into Heaven to the Father's throne, skipping over His ministry on the earth, His death, and resurrection. The panoramic vision moves to the middle of the tribulation period, when Israel will be forced to leave the Promised Land for the last half of that seven-year period (1,260 days). The time scheme of verses 4–6 thus skips over the Church Age and the first half of the Tribulation.

The War

In the middle of the Tribulation, a war will occur between Michael and Satan and their respective angelic armies. Satan will lose and be forced to earth (12:7–9).

His descent and concentrated activities on earth will produce a mixed reaction. The inhabitants of Heaven, including angels and redeemed men, will rejoice, but a woe is pronounced upon earth's inhabitants (12:10–12). This woe is the third woe, or the sounding of the seventh trumpet. Satan will know that he has but a short time, the last half of the Tribulation, to resist and oppose God.

18. Read Revelation 11:10–12. For what did the loud voice tell the heavenly citizens to rejoice?

The Persecution

Satan will then pour out his wrath upon the woman, Israel, in the last half of the Tribulation (12:13–17). God will providentially protect her in the wilderness for "a time, and times, and half a time" (12:14). This unique phrase is synonymous with 1,260 days, three and one-half years, or forty-two months. Frustrated in his attempt to destroy the woman, he then turns upon "the remnant of her seed" (12:17), conceivably a reference to believing Jews who live throughout the kingdom of the Antichrist.

19. Read Revelation 12:13–17. Why doesn't Satan ever give up in his fight against Christ?

20. How important to you is knowing that Christ will ultimately prevail and that the end of Satan is defeat?

Making It Personal

21. If the godly can praise God during the Tribulation, then you can find reasons to praise Him today. What are some reasons for you to praise God today?

22. Why should there never be a time when you can't think of anything to praise God for?

23. Commit to praise God for His promises regarding your future. Write a praise to Him right now.

24. Read Revelation 11:17.

The Beasts

*Even in the darkest of days,
God stands as the Sovereign.*

Revelation 13; 14

**"I heard a voice from heaven saying unto me,
Write, Blessed are the dead which die in the Lord
from henceforth: Yea, saith the Spirit, that they
may rest from their labours; and their works do
follow them" (Revelation 14:13).**

May 19, 1780 is known as "New England's Dark Day."
The sky over New England "was enveloped in darkness." In Rupert, New York, the darkness obscured the sun as early as
sunrise. "Extraordinary darkness" occurred midmorning and "continued
till the middle of the next night" in Cambridge, Massachusetts. Residents
of the country observed birds going to roost, cocks crowing at mid-
day, and "plainly terrified" animals. The darkness spread from Portland,
Maine, in the north to New Jersey in the south—all caused by the smoke
from massive forest fires in Ontario, Canada!

Getting Started

1. Identify the darkest place (physical, not spiritual) you have ever
visited. How did you feel while experiencing that darkness?

2. How valuable was a light source to you at that time?

Revelation 13 will present a very dark situation, while chapter 14 provides hope and assurance that God is firmly in control of all things.

Searching the Scriptures

The parenthesis between the seventh trumpet and the bowl judgments continues into this section (12:1—14:20). The fact of satanic hostility toward God and Israel has been discussed (Rev. 12). Now the visible, earthly means of the expression of that hatred will be seen through the Devil's control of the two beasts (Rev. 13). In this sense, a satanic league, a counterfeit trinity, is formed. Various announcements of judgment and blessing will subsequently be given to offset the terror of the wicked reign of the Antichrist (Rev. 14).

The First Beast's Person

The first beast to appear in Revelation 13 comes out of the sea. In prophetic Scripture, the sea represents the masses of sinful Gentile nations. In his vision-dream, Daniel saw beasts rise out of the sea (Dan. 7:1–8). Those beasts symbolized the rise of Gentile powers over the nation of Israel, as seen in the subsequent rules of Babylon, Persia, Greece, and Rome. The first beast, therefore, will be a Gentile.

The first beast has seven heads, upon which the name of blasphemy is imprinted (Rev. 13:1). Who or what are these seven heads? The most plausible view is that the heads depict the seven major national powers that have occupied the land of Israel: Egypt, Assyria, Babylon, Persia, Greece, Rome, and the kingdom of the Antichrist. The blasphemous names show their utter contempt for God and His covenant people. They repudiate divine sovereignty and ascribe the prerogatives of deity to themselves.

3. Read Revelation 13:1. What might people conclude about God as they watch the blasphemous beast rise to world dominance?

The beast from the sea has ten horns. These horns refer to the ten-nation confederation that will support the Antichrist in his seizure of power (Rev. 17:12–17). They are the same entity as the two feet, or ten toes, of Nebuchadnezzar's dream image and as the ten horns of the fourth beast in Daniel's vision. They seem to represent the nations of western Europe that are bound together in the European Economic Community. The ten crowns on the horns demonstrate their individual sovereignty, yet they are joined together in an alliance to support the rise of the Antichrist.

The beast has a body of a leopard, feet of a bear, and mouth of a lion to show he is a composite of past Gentile rulers and nations (13:2). In Daniel's vision, the prophet saw animals rise out of the sea in this order: lion, bear, leopard, and nondescript. All Gentile oppression of Israel thus finds its apex within the anti-Semitic nature of the Antichrist. He basically is the personification of all of the worst qualities of those nations.

Satan, the dragon, is the power behind the rise of the Antichrist. Satan gives him three things: his power, his seat (or throne), and his great authority (13:2). Just as the Father authenticated His Son, Jesus Christ, so Satan certifies his man in counterfeit deception.

4. Read Daniel 4:34–37. What did Nebuchadnezzar, whose kingdom was represented by the lion, conclude about God?

5. Read Daniel 5:18–23. What did Belshazzar, the last king of Babylon, fail to learn about God?

6. How does Daniel describe God in Daniel 5:23?

The First Beast's Activity

The unsaved will worship the beast (13:4). Paul declared that the Antichrist will represent himself as God when he establishes his throne within the temple of God in Jerusalem and when he bans all other forms of religious exercise (2 Thess. 2:4). The unregenerate will be so amazed at the counterfeit death and resurrection that they will ascribe deity to both Satan and the beast. Satan has always desired the worship of other creatures, and in the Tribulation he will have it.

7. Read Isaiah 14:12–14. What did Satan say he would do that showed his desire to be worshiped by all creation?

8. Read Matthew 4:8–10. How did Satan demonstrate his desire for worship while tempting Christ in the wilderness?

The world will be impressed with both the person and his power. But those who come to Christ during the Tribulation will recognize the deception and will refuse to worship the beast (Rev. 13:8).

9. What are the answers to the questions in Revelation 13:4?

The beast will blaspheme God and His people (13:5, 6). Specifically, he will attack the name of God and the heavenly tabernacle, the center of God's eternal rule in holiness. Further, he attacks the inhabitants of Heaven, including the holy angels and probably also the redeemed. He will go unopposed in his blasphemous charges for forty-two months, the second half of the Great Tribulation.

10. What will the false messiah no doubt conclude when his blasphemous charges go unopposed for forty-two months?

The beast will make war with the saints and will overcome them (13:7). The title "the saints" refers to believing Israel during the Tribulation. The Antichrist will betray the people of Israel and break his seven-year covenant with them (Dan. 9:24–27). By so doing, he will gain personal control of Jerusalem and the land of Israel as well as authority over the entire earth (Rev. 13:7).

11. Read Revelation 13:7. What must the beast think of himself as he brazenly takes over Israel and takes power over the entire world?

12. Read Revelation 13:8. How will all those who have the mark of the beast respond to his world domination?

John records an exhortation to the reader in verse 9 and 10. Though similar to earlier admonitions to the seven churches, it lacks one important phrase—"unto the churches." The true church will be in Heaven when the Antichrist reveals himself; therefore, this exhortation is for the tribulation believer. The believer must take courage from the fact that the Antichrist and his followers will not get away with their sinful actions.

13. Read Revelation 13:10. Summarize the message of this verse.

14. Read Deuteronomy 7:9, 10. What does this passage say about the sureness of God's vengeance?

The Second Beast's Person

The second beast in Revelation 13 came out of the earth (v. 11). He is called the false prophet. He has two horns like a lamb to give the appearance of being harmless. He is, however, a wolf sheep's clothing (Rev. 19:20; Matt. 7:15). He seems defenseless, yet he has two horns. The presence of horns in prophetic Scripture usually indicates spheres of rule; thus these horns may reveal religious authority.

The false prophet speaks as a dragon. Docile in appearance, he demonstrates satanic authority and power when he speaks. His word is law, and those who disobey it will be punished.

His Activity

The second beast has the same satanically given power as the first beast. He exercises the power to direct worship toward the first beast (13:12–15). Through deceiving miracles, he forces the unsaved inhabitants of the earth to worship the Antichrist and to erect an image of the Antichrist. He then animates the manufactured icon to speak. The real object of the false religion is Satan himself.

15. Read Revelation 13:15. What is the consequence of not worshiping the beast?

The false prophet also uses Satan's power to perform miracles (13:13). His most spectacular accomplishment will be to call fire down from heaven in the presence of onlookers. This miraculous display rivals and simulates the powers demonstrated by the two witnesses (11:5, 6).

Furthermore, the false prophet uses Satan's power to control commerce (13:16–18). In a devastated world where food will be both scarce and expensive (6:5, 6), the second beast will control the religious wills of people by the rationing of food. If they want to eat, they will need to worship the beast.

In the area of commerce the false prophet has power over all strata of society. He requires an identification mark to be imprinted on either the right hand or the forehead to qualify a person for the distribution of food. In essence the people place their trust in Satan for their food.

The mark is the number 666, the number of man. Man was created on the sixth day. This number represents the deification of man in total rebellion against the triune God. The climax of total depravity will occur when people will worship a man as their god. Verse 18 closes with an exhortation to recognize that 666 is the number of man.

Chapter 13 can give the reader the impression that the evil trinity is in absolute control. That control, if it were truly absolute, would produce a dark and disheartening situation. However, Revelation 14 anticipates the ultimate triumph of God and sets forth His triumph in a series of six announcements, or declarations.

Reason for Hope: The 144,000

The 144,000 are with Jesus Christ on Mount Zion (14:1). This mount could refer to earthly Jerusalem or to the heavenly mount. If the scene is Jerusalem, then this vision is an anticipation of the millennial Kingdom when God will establish His Son as the King of Israel and of the world. If it is the heavenly mount, then the 144,000 have probably been martyred and are now in Heaven with the Savior. At this point in the book, the second view seems more plausible.

16. What hope is seen in the appearance of the 144,000?

Reason for Hope: Angelic Preacher

God presently uses human beings to evangelize lost mankind, but in the second half of the Tribulation, He will use an angel to proclaim the gospel (14:6). With the two witnesses and 144,000 gone, God will give the world one last chance to hear the truth of redemption. The threefold command is simple and direct: Fear God and give glory to and worship the Creator (14:7).

17. How does the angelic preacher signify hope?

Reason for Hope: Fall of Babylon

Revelation 14:8 has the first mention of Babylon in Revelation. The double mention of the verb "is fallen" indicates divine certainty of judgment. It may also show a double portion of judgment (18:6). Two reasons are given for her punishment: her own spiritual fornication (17:4) and the spread of her sin to others (17:2).

18. What hope is there in the fall of Babylon?

Reason for Hope: Doom of the Beast Worshipers

The unregenerate who worship the beast and the image and who receive the mark of the beast will be confirmed in their unbelief (14:9). They will commit the unpardonable sin of the great tribulation period. They thus will be unable to be saved after their willful, blasphemous action.

Their punishment will be fourfold. They will experience God's undiluted wrath, which will be poured out in the bowl judgments and at Armageddon (14:10a). They will be tormented with fire and brimstone in the Lake of Fire for all eternity (14:10b; 21:8). They will experience endless torment. And they will have no rest from their pain and suffering (4:11). Again, John pointed out that these judgments are reserved for the worshipers of the beast.

19. What hope is seen in the revelation of the doom of the beast worshipers?

Reason for Hope: Blessedness of the Saved

The principles in Revelation 14:12 and 13 have their primary application to the believers of the Tribulation, and in a secondary sense, to believers of all ages. Believers have the assurance that their unsaved persecutors will receive eternal, divine punishment. Also, a blessedness marks the death of a believer, especially a genuine martyrdom (14:13). God will refresh His children and reward them in their conscious existence after death (14:13).

20. What hope is seen in the message about the blessing on the saved?

Reason for Hope: Harvest of the Earth

Two harvests are mentioned in Revelation 14:14–20. One interpretation is that the first harvest refers to the salvation of living Gentiles in the second half of the Tribulation and the second harvest to the judgment of the wicked at Armageddon. A second possibility is that the first harvest refers to the removal of the living unsaved from earth (the tares; Matt. 13:38–42) and the second harvest, to the destruction of the wicked rebels (19:11–21).

The imagery of the winepress (Rev. 14:20) compares the destruction to the land of Palestine, which is about 200 miles long. The Battle of Armageddon will cover all the land, with the central section being the valley of Megiddo (Joel 3:11–16). Unsaved men are equated with ripe grapes who are trampled by the second coming of Jesus Christ (Rev. 19:15).

21. What hope is seen in the harvest of the earth?

Making It Personal

22. Which of the reasons for hope in Revelation 14 are available to believers today?

23. Does God provide a sufficient number of reasons for you to hope in Him to meet even the darkest need in your life?

24. Choose a need in your life (or one in a friend's life) and relate it to one or more of the reasons for hope identified above. Compose a prayer of trust and hope. Then pray this prayer to God, Who controls the present as well as the future.

24. Memorize Revelation 14:13.

The Bowl Judgments

God's wrath is based on His righteous character.

Revelation 15; 16

"And they sing the song of Moses the servant of God, and the song of the Lamb, saying, Great and marvellous are thy works, Lord God Almighty; just and true are thy ways, thou King of saints" (Revelation 15:3).

The Spanish Empire was one of the first modern global empires. It began with the reign of Queen Isabella and her husband Ferdinand—the people who financed Christopher Columbus's voyage in 1492. Queen Isabella reorganized her kingdom's system of government, lowered its crime rate, and pulled it out of enormous debt. It is not surprising that the competent woman who took these actions was a woman of personal character. The historian Andres Bernaldez said of Isabella: "She was an endeavored woman, very powerful, very prudent, wise, very honest, chaste, devout, discreet, truthful, clear, without deceit."

Getting Started

1. List several professions in which character is as important as competency.

2. Why does character count?

God always acts based on His righteous character. Revelation 15 and 16 demonstrate that God always acts based on His righteous character. Even His judgments on the earth are pure and righteous.

Searching the Scriptures

The lengthy parenthesis between the trumpet and the bowl judgments is now over (12:1—14:20). The final series of seven judgments is about to begin.

Another Heavenly Sign

John saw another heavenly sign (15:1). This phenomenon corresponds to the other two signs that he had seen: the woman (12:1) and the dragon (12:3). To John's eyes, the sign was "great" in its outward, objective scope; it was also "marvellous" in that it produced an inward, emotional response of awe and admiration.

The sign John saw was the seven angels with the seven last plagues. In them "is filled up the wrath of God" (15:1). The Greek root word for the verb "is filled up" is the same that Christ used when He exclaimed, "It is finished" (John 19:30). The mystery of God (Rev. 10:7) will also be "finished" (same word) in the sounding of the seventh trumpet. The outpourings of divine wrath, contained within the seals, the trumpets, and the bowls will reach their completion in these seven last plagues.

Tribulation Martyrs

John then saw the tribulation martyrs standing on the sea of glass, which lies before the heavenly throne of God (15:2). The martyrs are the ones who have overcome the beast and his image, mark, and number. In the earthly sense, the beast overcomes them by killing them, but actually they are victorious over him (12:11). John saw and heard these victors singing the praises of God (15:3, 4).

3. Read Revelation 15:3, 4. What aspects of God's character are referred to in this passage?

Revelation 15:3 is reflected in Moses' swan song to the children of Israel as he challenged them before they crossed over the Jordan to possess the Promised Land. God judged Moses for his disobedience and told him that he would not possess the land despite years of leading God's people.

4. Read Deuteronomy 32:3, 4. What might you have expected Moses to sing about God considering he was not allowed to enter the Promised Land?

Opened Temple, Great Voice

John then saw the "temple" opened, that is, the inner sanctuary of the heavenly tabernacle, or the Holy of Holies (Rev. 15:5). He had seen it opened in the sounding of the seventh trumpet (11:19). This observation provides further support for the view that the seven bowl angels are revealed during the sounding of the seventh trumpet. Their garments of pure white linen fastened by golden girdles seem to symbolize righteousness and royalty. God is the king of the universe, and He will judge on the basis of moral rightness.

5. Read Revelation 15:8. What evidence in this verse points to the righteousness of God as the bowls of His wrath are brought out?

One of the four living creatures then gives to the seven angels the seven golden vials, or bowls. No angel or man can enter the temple during the outpouring of the seven bowl judgments (15:8).

John then heard a great voice from within the smoke-filled temple (16:1). The voice commanded the seven angels with the seven bowls to pour out the divine wrath upon the earth (16:1). The bowl judgments, briefly described in the Scriptures, seem to be poured out in succession during the second half of the tribulation period.

First Bowl

The outpouring of the first bowl produces "a noisome and grievous" sore upon both those who have the mark of the beast and those who worship the image of the beast (16:2). The sore has an internal, cancerous quality; but it is also on the outside of the body, quite observable, and possibly contagious. This divinely imposed sore cannot be cured by human medicine or satanic miracles. It seems to last throughout the duration of the bowl judgments (16:11).

6. Why is illness a particularly troubling judgment?

Second Bowl

The outpouring of the second bowl causes the sea literally to become blood as of a dead person (16:3). There is legitimate dispute as to the scope of the sea. Does it refer to the Mediterranean Sea, the Sea of Galilee, some large ocean, or to all saltwater oceans? No dogmatic position can be held here.

7. What would be some repercussions from this judgment?

Third Bowl

The outpouring of the third bowl affects freshwater rivers and fountains, or springs (16:4). They also become blood. This punitive action brings a double response from the angel of the waters and the angel of the altar (16:5–7).

8. Read Revelation 16:5–7. What do the angels recognize about the character of God?

9. What does the angel of the waters recognize about the people on whom this plague fell (v. 6)?

Both angels acknowledge God's character: His sovereign lordship, His righteousness, His eternality, His truth, and His moral right to judge. Since the unsaved have shed the blood of God's people, God is just in giving blood as the drink of the unregenerate.

Fourth Bowl

The fourth trumpet lessened the heat of the sun, but the outpouring of the fourth bowl will intensify the heat of the sun (16:8, 9). The angel will scorch men with great heat through the sun. Although this judgment apparently affects the entire inhabited earth, there is no indication that the saved will receive this severe sunburn. The twofold response to the great heat further supports the contention that only the unsaved are involved.

10. Read Revelation 16:8, 9. How do the unsaved respond to this bowl?

11. What are they showing about their beliefs regarding God's wrath?

People in tribulation will recognize the fact that God is greater than the sun and that He has used the sun to manifest His power. In itself, this fact should be sufficient to produce genuine confession of sin and repentance; however, these unsaved remain firm in their unbelief.

Fifth Bowl

The outpouring of the fifth bowl produces a darkness throughout the kingdom of the Antichrist (Rev 16:10, 11). It apparently first comes upon the seat, or literally, the "throne" of the beast. This is a reference to his capital, either Rome or Jerusalem, probably the latter because he establishes his throne within the Jewish temple in the middle of the Tribulation. This darkness then spreads out from the throne to all the borders of the kingdom.

This phenomenon produces three reactions by the unsaved. They gnaw their tongues in pain because of the earlier imposed sore, they blaspheme God again because of their physical discomfort, and they do not repent of their sinful deeds.

12. What three words would you use to describe the judged at this point?

13. What three words might the judged use to describe God?

Sixth Bowl

The outpouring of the sixth bowl is directed specially at the Euphrates River (16:12). This river flows seventeen hundred miles from its source into the Persian Gulf. It forms the eastern boundary of the land area promised to the nation of Israel through Abraham (Gen. 15:18). It is a natural barrier between the Middle East and the breadth of land that stretches toward the Far East.

The sixth bowl judgment causes the Euphrates to dry up so that its channel becomes a dry riverbed. Consequently, the kings of the east are able to move into the heartland of the Middle East. Daniel prophesied that "tidings from the east" would disturb the Antichrist (Dan. 11:44). The darkness imposed upon the kingdom of the Antichrist will permit the eastern kings to move across the land bridge from the Far East to the Euphrates River. These eastern kings probably refer to China and her satellite friends.

Parenthesis

In all of the three series (seals, trumpets, bowls) there is a parenthetical insertion of material between the sixth and the seventh judgments. The bowls are no exception (16:13–16).

John saw three unclean spirits like frogs coming respectively out of the mouths of the dragon (Satan), the beast (Antichrist), and the false prophet. They are identified as demonic spirits, performing satanic miracles. They are instrumental in influencing the kings of the world to congregate in Israel for the final battle—the war between man and God (16:14).

14. What must the armies of the earth think of God in order to rally together to go to battle against Him?

15. What must they think of themselves to think they are able to win?

Armageddon, literally the hill of Megiddo, encompasses the valley (fourteen miles wide and twenty miles long) that will occupy the central position of the battle.

At this time, Christ predicts that He will come as a thief unannounced. He pronounces a blessing upon the tribulation believers who will be watching for Him and who will be living godly lives (16:15).

Seventh Bowl

When the seventh bowl is poured out upon the air, apparently above the congregated armies within Israel, the great temple voice declares, "It is done" (16:17). This verb literally means "it has come to be." The judgments of God, from the first seal to the seventh bowl, are now history.

The judgment produces a mammoth earthquake (16:18). This unprecedented shaking divides Jerusalem, the great city, into three parts (16:19). The cities of the nations with their tall buildings will collapse to the ground. Babylon, whose judgment is described in detail in the following chapters (17:1—18:24) is singled out for special divine wrath. The earthquake will reduce mountains to landslides and will cause a tidal wave that will destroy the islands. In addition, great hail (weighing 110–125 pounds) will rain upon the earth.

16. Read Revelation 16:21. How did the unsaved react to the last judgment from God?

17. What is your reaction to their continued disrespect for God?

The response of the unsaved to these divine phenomena remains unchanged. They continue to blaspheme God.

Making It Personal

18. Why are you thankful that God's anger is based on His righteous character?

19. What would life be like with an almighty god without righteous character?

20. What value is God's righteous character to believers today?

21. Offer a prayer of praise to God for His righteous character, keeping in mind your present circumstances.

22. Memorize Revelation 15:3.

The Fall of Babylon

When God decides it is time, judgment comes.

Revelation 17:1—19:6

"I heard as it were the voice of a great multitude, and as the voice of many waters, and as the voice of mighty thunderings, saying, Alleluia: for the Lord God omnipotent reigneth" (Revelation 19:6)

Why do criminals keep committing the same crimes over and over again? In large part they are delusional and think that they will never get caught. Even those who do get caught will continue to commit crimes once they are out of jail. As many as forty percent of them land back in prison.

Getting Started

1. Can a criminal, or any other sinner for that matter, ever truly say he will never get caught? Explain.

2. Why might some people have an "I'll never get caught" attitude when it comes to their sins?

Babylon is the focus of this lesson. Babylon leaves no doubt that it deserves God's judgment. They cannot escape. When God decides it is time, His judgment comes.

Searching the Scriptures

After the outpouring of the bowl judgments, there is a lengthy insertion of content dealing with the influence of Babylon and her subsequent destruction.

The term "Babylon" must be seen as both a literal city and a religious-political-commercial system. The fall of Babylon is announced earlier in the book (14:8; 16:19). Chapters 17 and 18 give a vivid description of the destruction of her religious-political influence and her commercial clout.

Two major symbols are portrayed in this chapter, the harlot and the beast. The same beast is described earlier and identified as the Antichrist with his empire (11:7; 13:1–10). Babylon is earlier depicted by name and as a great city (14:8; 16:19), but now her true nature is disclosed.

The Woman

One of the seven angels who poured out the bowl judgments charged John to come and see the judgment of Babylon (17:1).

Babylon is called a "great whore." This word, often translated as "harlot" or "prostitute," is used for the concept of fornication. In this context, Babylon's harlotry is of a corporate spiritual nature; she has violated the principle of moral fidelity toward the true God. If this woman is the apostate ecclesiastical system of the tribulation era, then the term "harlot" vividly portrays her ethical degeneration.

3. What are some of the Biblical absolutes that the apostate church will obviously deny?

4. What will be some of the ethical degeneration that will go along with denying Biblical absolutes?

The woman sits upon "many waters" (17:1b). These waters are later interpreted as "peoples, and multitudes, and nations, and tongues" (17:15). This concept suggests that her power extends to all parts of the populated earth.

5. Why should Bible-believing, fundamental churches resist joining forces with liberal churches even if their combined efforts would accomplish something good?

The kings of the earth have an illicit political association with the woman (17:2a). It would appear that the leaders of many nations court her favor and are willing to violate divine standards in so doing.

6. Why would the political leaders want to court the woman's favor?

The woman adversely influences "the inhabitants of the earth" (17:2b). She motivates ordinary citizens to do that which is evil. She herself is sinful, and she wants others to join her.

The woman is associated with the beast, the Antichrist (17:3). Since she "sits" upon the beast, the impression is that she controls him and all his power. The beast thus supports her and seems to be carrying her to her chosen purpose and destination. This strange alignment probably occurs during the first half of the Tribulation, but after the beast assumes full autocratic powers, he destroys her during the second half of the Tribulation.

7. When have you seen a politician or leader use religion to get ahead politically?

Verse four relates that the woman is wealthy (17:4). The costly clothing and jewelry speak of her glory and extravagance. Her golden chalice is full of spiritual wickedness.

She has a unique name: "MYSTERY, BABYLON THE GREAT, THE MOTHER OF HARLOTS AND ABOMINATIONS OF THE EARTH" (17:5). According to Biblical definition, a mystery is a truth not known or revealed in the Old Testament but now revealed through the apostles and their writings. The name "Babylon," therefore, cannot refer merely to the ancient Mesopotamian city and kingdom. As used in the context of new truth contained in the book of Revelation, it must denote a city and system that has been given symbolic significance by God. In the first century, the woman represented both the city and empire of Rome. She is identified as the great city which "reigneth" over the kings of the earth (17:18). In the era of John the apostle, that city had to be Rome.

The name "Babylon" is attached to Rome because the original Babylon became the starting point for organized political and religious rebellion against God (Gen. 10:8–10; 11:1–9).

The identification of Babylon with Rome is further substantiated by the fact that the city and the woman both sit on seven mountains (17:9). The poets of Rome frequently referred to her as the city of seven hills. The mystery nature of the name seems to point to a concentration of religious and political power that can also be localized in an observable city. Most evangelical spokesmen prefer the interpretation that "Mystery Babylon" refers to organized Christendom in the Tribulation embracing apostate liberalism.

8. Read Revelation 17:6. What might life be like for a Tribulation believer under the rule of such an evil religious system?

The woman is understandably an adversary of God's people (17:6). Her antagonism is aimed at both Jews and Gentiles.

Genuine believers will wonder at the woman's existence and influence (17:6, 7). John's awe is expressive of what the saints will express in the Tribulation.

9. What do these descriptions of the woman suggest about the need for a righteous God to bring judgment on Babylon?

The Beast

John stared with wonder at the sight of the great harlot, but in the Tribulation, the unsaved will marvel at the uniqueness of the beast (17:8). Their names were not written in the Book of Life before time began. At the Great White Throne Judgment, the absence of their names shows that they never were saved (20:12, 15).

10. Read Revelation 17:8. Do you marvel at the descriptions and abilities of the beast? Explain.

The beast's origin and control are satanic (17:8). His ascent out of the demonic abyss and his destination of perdition show the wickedness of the beastly king and his empire (11:7). The past, present, and future qualities of his existence probably refer to the rise of the Roman Empire, its collapse, and its eventual reconstruction under the leadership of the Antichrist.

The seven heads of the beast have a double prophetic significance (17:9–11). They represent the seven mountains on which the woman sits (17:9, 18). Since the city that ruled the earth in the time of John was Rome, the seven mountains must be interpreted as seven literal hills.

However, the mountains also have a symbolic interpretation. They signify kings or kingdoms (17:10, 11). These mountains/kingdoms picture the empires that have conquered and oppressed the nation of Israel since its inception. The one mountain/kingdom which "is" (signifying present existence) must refer to the power of Rome in the first century, the era in which John lived and wrote. The future mountain/kingdom points to the last Gentile world power, the kingdom of the Antichrist during the tribulation period.

11. Read Revelation 17:10, 11. What phrases in these verses show that the kingdom of the beast will not survive God's judgment?

The beast's time of control over Israel is limited. This period of three and one-half years of domination over Jerusalem is indeed short when compared to the decades and hundreds of years exercised by the former Gentile nations. The beast, the person of the ruler, now is seen as the eighth kingdom, which will arise out of the revived Roman federation.

The ten horns on the beast portray the ten-nation confederation that will form the nucleus of the rule of the Antichrist (17:12–14). In prophetic Scripture they correspond to the ten horns that arise out of the fourth beast (namely Rome) in Daniel's vision of the future (Dan. 7:7, 8, 20, 24). They also correspond to the ten toes of the iron feet mixed with clay (which are an extension of the iron legs) of the dream-image of Nebuchadnezzar (Dan. 2:41–44).

In the first century, this ten-nation power did not exist ("which have received no kingdom as yet"; v. 12). Its influence will not be felt until the Antichrist rises to power in the future Tribulation (17:12). Its entire purpose for existence will be to support the Antichrist (17:13). The ten-nation confederation will make a fatal mistake when it attempts to make war with Christ, the Lamb (17:14a). This event occurs at Armageddon (19:19).

12. Read Revelation 17:14. What is the name given for Christ in the description of His military victory?

13. Why is that name particularly appropriate at the battle of Armageddon?

In total obedience to the desire of the beast, the ten-horn confederation will hate the great harlot, will throw her off its back, and will utterly destroy her (17:16). The Antichrist will establish himself as the absolute dictator and god of the world.

14. Read Revelation 17:17. How do you see the sovereignty of God at work in this verse?

Judgment on Babylon

There is an honest difference of opinion over the identity of Babylon mentioned in chapters 18 and 19. Some claim that the Mystery Babylon of chapter 17 refers to political-ecclesiastical Rome; whereas, the destroyed Babylon of Revelation 18 is the literal, commercial power of rebuilt Babylon on the Euphrates. Since there seems to be a strong continuity between the two chapters, it is more plausible to see two different aspects of the same prophetic entity.

John saw an angel of power and glory descend from Heaven with the announcement of accomplished judgment against Babylon (18:1, 2). The repeated verb phrase "is fallen" indicates divine certainty and finality.

Babylon was demonic in character, one reason for her fall (18:2). The true church is the dwelling place of the Holy Spirit (Eph. 2:22), but this apostate ecclesiastical-political system will be the habitation of evil spirits.

15. What might demonic influence in a church look like today?

A second reason for Babylon's fall was her influence on the world
to participate in her sin (Rev. 18:3). Her adverse affect on political leaders and her use of her influence for indulgent gain are the final two reasons for her fall (18:3).

God has always called His people to separation from false religious
organizations (2 Cor. 6:14—7:1). In the Tribulation, it will be no different. Here is a clarion call for tribulation saints—perhaps an exclusive
reference to the nation of Israel—to separate from the structure of Babylon lest they share in the physical punishment (Rev. 18:4).

John records the justification for judgment on Babylon. The first is
she has excessive sins (18:5). Furthermore, she is only reaping what she
has sown (18:6). Finally, she is involved in proud, arrogant self-indul-
gence (18:7, 8). No nation or individual can defy God indefinitely.

Mourning

Three major groups lament the destruction of Babylon. The first
group to express mourning is the kings of the earth (18:9, 10). These
kings, mentioned earlier in their association with the harlot (17:2), are
different from the ten kings aligned with the beast (17:12, 16). The latter
delight in the destruction of Babylon; whereas, these kings lament because they profited from her prosperity.

The second group of mourners is "the merchants of the earth"
(18:11–17a). They lament for two selfish reasons—the reduction of the
sale of their merchandise (18:11–14) and the decrease of their personal
wealth (18:15). They identify themselves with her in the time of glory
and prosperity, but they want nothing to do with her torment and punishment.

The third group is the sea merchants, including shipmasters, sail-
ors, and ship owners (18:17–19). The great commercial loss suffered by
these groups demonstrates that the harlot has great economic power in
the first half of the Tribulation.

Rejoicing

16. Read Revelation 18:20. Why should the godly rejoice at the fall of Babylon? For what still future event does it pave the way?

The voice which described the fall of Babylon (18:4–19) now calls upon the godly to rejoice at the fall (18:20). The destruction of Babylon is necessary to prepare the way for the return of Christ.

The majority of the inhabitants of the earth will mourn over the fall of Babylon, but the dwellers in Heaven will unanimously rejoice over her destruction. The command to rejoice is based upon the completion of divine vengeance (18:20). Its finality is depicted in the casting of the millstone into the sea (18:21).

17. Read Revelation 18:21–23. What repeated phrase demonstrates that Babylon's doom is final?

Two more reasons for her severe devastation are given. First, she deceived the nations with her "sorceries," a term that can be transliterated as "pharmacies," a reference to drugs and the occult (18:23). Second, she was morally and judicially liable for the martyrdom of the righteous (18:24).

The command to rejoice (18:20) is now followed by the response (19:1–6). Four movements of joy are delineated in the response. First, there is the "great voice of much people in heaven" (19:1). This "people," conceivably, are the same group identified earlier as the tribulation martyrs (7:9, 10). They verbalize "alleluia," meaning "praise ye the Lord." The significance of this term's now being sung in Heaven is that Christ, the rejected yet anointed King of the earth, is about to return the glory of God to the earth in the person of Himself (19:11–16). It is no wonder that Heaven shouts with praise.

Second, the elders and the living creatures jointly prostrate them-selves before God in worship and vocal adoration (19:4). Third, the throne voice charges the servants of God and all those who fear God to praise Him (19:5). Fourth, the voice of the great multitude probably be-longs to the 144,000 Jews (14:1–5). They also praise God in anticipation of the millennial, eternal reign of Christ (19:6).

Making It Personal

18. What warnings for your present life can you draw from the yet future but sure destruction of Babylon?

19. What can individuals do to remove God's just judgment from their lives?

20. Are any of the sins leveled against Babylon present in your life?

21. Consider an appropriate personal response to the truth of God's sure and just judgment on sin.

22. Memorize Revelation 19:6.

The Second Coming of Christ

*Christ will return as King of Kings
and Lord of Lords.*

Revelation 19:7–21

"And he hath on his vesture and on his thigh a name written, KING OF KINGS, AND LORD OF LORDS" (Revelation 19:16).

There is no such thing as a perfect wedding. Everyone who has been married can tell about something that went wrong in their wedding. One horse-loving bride had a pre-wedding picture taken with her favorite horse. The horse grabbed her bouquet after just one picture and took off across a pasture. When the horse was finally tracked down he had eaten half of the bouquet. The horse's pink teeth proved he was guilty. A quick-thinking bridesmaid repaired the bouquet for the wedding.

Getting Started

1. Describe a wedding, perhaps your own, that didn't go exactly as planned.

2. What is your idea of a perfect wedding?

All believers will one day be involved in the absolutely perfect wedding. The church will be the bride of Christ. Revelation 19, part of this lesson's focus, presents that perfect day. We should live now in such a way to prepare for that day.

Searching the Scriptures

The lengthy discussion of the Great Tribulation is now over (4:1—19:6). In the next four chapters, John will see the final eight prophetic events in rapid succession. These events will be pointed out by the repeated use of the phrase "And I saw" (19:11, 17, 19; 20:1, 4, 11, 12; 21:1, 2, 22). John thus saw the future as God sees it—as established historical events.

Clothing for the Marriage of the Lamb

A double charge is given to believers: subjectively to rejoice, and objectively to give honor to Jesus Christ (19:7). The occasion for this appeal is the imminence of the marriage of the Lamb. This marriage will take place in Heaven just before Christ descends to the earth. The presence of the wife in Heaven serves as another argument for the pretribulational rapture of the church.

3. Read Revelation 19:7, 8. What makes up our garments as the bride of Christ?

4. How will your life on earth affect that garment?

The clothing of the bride involves both the imputed righteousness of God in Christ and the righteous deeds of believers. The former is the positional clothing of the church; whereas, the latter stresses the practice of the saints. When a sinner believes solely upon Christ for his salvation (Acts 16:31), he becomes part of the bride of the Lamb.

The clothing of the bride is described as "fine linen, clean and white." The linen is further defined as "the righteousness of saints." This suggests the righteous deeds of the believers. The preparation of the bride takes place at the Bema, or Judgment Seat of Christ, where Christ will reward the church for its righteous acts (2 Cor. 5:10).

The bride therefore has a double garment: the wedding garment of imputed righteousness given to her at the moment of conversion, and the clean, white linen awarded to her by Christ.

Blessing of the Supper

Although many equate the marriage of the lamb with the marriage supper of the lamb, they should be seen as two distinct events. The marriage of the lamb is between Christ and the true church, and it will take place in Heaven just before the second advent. The marriage supper, on the other hand, will occur on earth at the outset of the Millennium. The "called" are the Old Testament saints, the tribulation believers, and possibly the holy angels. Since no earthly bride needs to be invited to her own wedding reception, the analogy in this passage would exclude the New Testament church saints as wedding guests. Christ Himself promised that He would eat and drink with His own after the Kingdom of God was established (Luke 22:14–18). This wedding feast, thus, must take place on earth after Christ returns to set up the Kingdom.

5. How refreshing is it to read of an event on earth that will include joy and complete harmony?

6. Do you have a place reserved at the table? If not, trust Christ as your Savior while there is time.

Essence of True Worship

7. Read Revelation 19:10. How did John respond to the announcement concerning the marriage supper?

The study of Biblical prophecy should always issue in genuine worship of God and greater adoration of Jesus Christ. God never gave the prophetic Word to satisfy the curiosity of natural minds. When a believer wants to view the future, he should always focus on the centrality of Jesus Christ. The "testimony of Jesus is the spirit of prophecy."

Second Coming of Christ

For two thousand years since His crucifixion, resurrection, and ascension, Christ has been in Heaven (Acts 1:9–11).

8. How might the unsaved respond to a two thousand year delay in the return of Christ?

9. Read 2 Peter 3:4. What did Peter record concerning how some of the lost of his day responded to the delay in Christ's return?

To the unregenerate mind, this lengthy delay indicates that the second coming of Jesus Christ is a fallacious tradition. They sneer and arrogantly laugh out, "Where is the promise of his coming?" (2 Pet. 3:4). The

Lord, however, is truth; thus, He always speaks the truth. Jesus Christ
will return to the earth, but He will come in His time. His delay is actually a blessing in disguise to the unsaved because it gives them another
opportunity to repent (2 Pet. 3:9).

His Description

At His first advent, Christ sat upon a donkey when He rode into Jerusalem (Zech. 9:9; Matt. 21:5). He then came in humility to save. At His
second advent, however, He will ride upon a white horse, signifying His
intent to judge and to triumph in war (Rev. 19:11).

10. Read Revelation 19:11. Why are the names Faithful and True important for believers?

11. Why should those same names cause the lost to fear?

Christ is designated as Faithful and True. The book earlier identified
Him in this way (1:5; 3:7). He is truth; therefore, He always speaks that
which God the Father wants Him to proclaim. His actions and speech
manifest His Being. He comes to judge and to make war in the sphere
of righteousness. His fiery eyes speak of His penetrating discernment
and judgment (Rev. 19:12; Heb. 4:12, 13). He knows the difference between the wheat and the tares, the good fish and the bad fish, the saved
and the false professors (Matt. 13).

Christ's robe dipped in blood is most likely a sign of His victory
(Rev. 19:13). The blood is from His enemies. The certainty of His victory
over them is foreshadowed by His riding to the battle with the blood already on His robe. Isaiah wrote of the blood splattered on Christ's robe
in Isaiah 63:1–4.

Christ's revealed name is the "Word of God" (Rev. 19:13; cf. John
1:1–3). In human language, words are symbols or communicators of

thoughts and concepts. Jesus Christ not only spoke the word of God; He was and is the Word of God. Whatever God is, Christ is. Only He could proclaim that to see Him is to see the Father (John 14:9).

12. Read Colossians 1:19. What did Paul write concerning Christ and the Father?

His Armies

Since both angels and redeemed humans will be clothed in clean, white linen (Rev. 15:6; 19:8), it is difficult to determine the exact composition of the heavenly armies (19:14). Since the word is in the plural ("armies") rather than the singular ("army"), it could include both groups. Christ predicted that angels would accompany Him at His second advent (Matt. 25:31), and in the immediate context, the Bride of the Lamb has been prepared for the descent (Rev. 19:7, 8). Nothing in Scripture indicates that these heavenly armies will be engaged in actual conflict. Christ alone will defeat His foes with the power of His spoken word.

13. What thoughts come to your mind as you consider accompanying Christ at His second coming?

His Actions

Isaiah wrote concerning the Messiah, "He shall smite the earth with the rod of his mouth, and with the breath of his lips shall he slay the wicked" (Isa. 11:4). In John's visions the power of Christ's word is symbolized by a sharp sword proceeding out of His mouth (Rev. 1:16; 2:12, 16). No actual, physical, prolonged conflict will occur between Christ and the evil trinity of Satan, the Antichrist, and the false prophet. All Christ will do is to speak, and His adversaries will collapse before Him (Rev. 19:15).

14. Why might the armies of the earth think they actually have a chance to defeat Christ?

15. How should you respond now to the fact that the lost will be hopeless before Christ?

Christ will be a Shepherd-King in the millennial Kingdom (19:15). He will rule the nations with a rod of iron (Ps. 2:9). His authority will be firm yet gentle.

When Christ descends to the earth, He will tread upon the unregenerate in the winepress of the wrath of God (Rev.14:19, 20; 19:15). He will stomp the very life out of them. From the divine perspective one reason that Christ has not yet returned is that the fruit (grapes) of human sin is not yet fully ripe. His second coming will also bring to an abrupt end the time of Gentile dominion over the nation of Israel (Luke 21:24).

Christ will come to assert Himself as the King of Kings and Lord of Lords (Rev. 19:16). The many crowns on His head will signify His rule over all (19:12).

Armageddon—Call to the Birds

The first mention of Armageddon, "the battle of that great day of God Almighty," was found in the parenthesis between the sixth and the seventh bowls (16:13–16). Revelation 19:17–21 simply gives the results of the battle, not the movements of armies or the actual sequence of conflict. This battle is the ultimate conflict between earth and Heaven, the clash between humanity and God.

Two suppers are set forth in this chapter: the marriage supper of the Lamb (19:9) and the supper of the great God (19:17). The first is a supper of life and joy; whereas, the second is a supper of judgment and death. When the living unsaved in the Tribulation reject the invitation to the first supper, they will be consumed in the second.

16. Who do you need to "invite" to join you at the first supper?

A holy angel will summon the birds to eat the flesh of the dead corpses before the battle is even waged. For the birds, it will indeed be a banquet of "flesh." In his prophecy, Ezekiel declared that both birds and beasts would devour the flesh of the invading northern armies (Ezek. 39:17–20), but that invasion will take place before the climax of Armageddon, discussed in this passage.

Armageddon—The Two Armies

Armageddon must be seen as the climax of a campaign by major powers to seize the land of Israel rather than as an isolated battle. It is difficult to trace the movements of armies during the Tribulation, but three major movements are foretold in Scripture.

The Tribulation begins with peace marked by a seven-year covenant of protection for Israel by the western confederation of nations ruled by the beast, namely the Antichrist (Dan. 9:27a). The northern (probably Russia) and the southern (Pan-Arab alliance and/or black Africa) powers will move against defenseless Israel (Ezek. 38; 39; Dan. 11:40). The Antichrist probably destroys the southern force (Dan. 11:41, 42); whereas, God directly judges the northern army (Ezek. 38:22, 23). The Antichrist will then break his covenant with Israel and will set himself up as a political-religious god (Dan. 9:27b). The armies of the east will then move toward the Promised Land (Rev. 16:12). Before the armies of the west and east collide, they will unite to fight against the descending Christ (16:14–16).

Doom of the Beast

Paul wrote that Christ will destroy the Antichrist with "the spirit of his mouth" and with "the brightness of his coming" (2 Thess. 2:8). The battle will be over as soon as Christ appears and opens His mouth (Rev. 19:20).

The beast and the false prophet will not die on the field of battle. They will not go to Hades (usually translated as "hell") to await the second resurrection of the lost. Rather, they will both be sent directly and alive ("living") into the Lake of Fire (19:20). They will not be consumed in the Lake of Fire; rather, they will experience eternal torment in a body divinely conditioned to endure such eternal fire. These two unregenerate men will be the first two individuals to be cast into the Lake of Fire. After the millennial Kingdom, Satan, the unholy angels, and all unsaved men will also be cast into it (Rev. 20:10, 14, 15; 21:8).

17. Why are the terrors of the Lake of Fire so hard to imagine?

18. How should you respond to the incomprehensible tortures of the Lake of Fire?

Destruction of the Armies

John then saw the actual destruction of the rebellious armies and the consumption of their flesh by the birds (19:21). Apparently, not all of the living unsaved at the end of the Tribulation will be killed or judged in this way. This radical death is reserved for members of the army units. When Christ sits upon the throne at the outset of His Kingdom, He will separate living Gentiles into the sheep (saved) and the goats (unsaved; Matt. 25:31–46). The unsaved will then be banished into eternal punishment.

Making It Personal

19. Review Revelation 19:11–21. What is your response as you consider Christ's judgment on humanity at His second coming?

20. How does the account help you see your need to share the gospel?

21. Who would you like to see saved before it is too late?

22. What two or three specific things could you do to encourage the salvation of those you listed?

23. Read Revelation 19:17.

The Millennium and the Great White Throne

Unrepentant sin brings eternal punishment.

Revelation 20

"Blessed and holy is he that hath part in the first resurrection: on such the second death hath no power, but they shall be priests of God and of Christ, and shall reign with him a thousand years" (Revelation 20:6).

Presidential candidates combine to raise over one billion dollars to communicate what they would do as president. Ironically the money they raise would go a long way toward solving the problems they claim they would fix as president. They could collectively give 10,000 people $100,000 each. It seems that becoming president is actually what they are most concerned about.

Getting Started

1. What would you do first if you got to be a ruler for a day?

2. What do you think you would like most about being a ruler?

3. What would you like least?

Being a ruler for a day is not just a dream; believers will have an opportunity to rule and reign with Christ in His millennial Kingdom. This lesson presents Christ's Kingdom, the final rebellion by Satan, and the final judgment of the lost.

Searching the Scriptures

We have now come to four major prophetic events, the last to occur before the creation of the new heaven and earth. They are briefly described in rapid sequence. They follow both a logical and a chronological order.

The beginning of the end for Satan happens when Michael and the holy angels force Satan to leave Heaven and to live on the earth at the middle of the Tribulation (12:7–13). On earth during the last three and one-half years he will energize the Antichrist. The second coming of Christ to the earth will change both the abode and the activity of Satan.

Satan's Confinement

John saw a holy angel descend out of Heaven, having the key of a bottomless pit and a great chain (20:1). The abyss is the place that evil spirits dread (Luke 8:31). It may be the equivalent of Tartarus (translated as "hell"; 2 Pet. 2:4), a site where evil angels are chained in darkness while they wait for their ultimate consignment to the Lake of Fire. It is possible that the abyss may be in the great gulf that was fixed between the place of torment and the place of comfort within Hades (Luke 16:26).

In the fifth trumpet judgment, God permits the abyss to be opened and the locusts to come forth out of the darkness (9:1–3). However, on the occasion recorded in chapter 20, God will direct the holy angel to open the abyss to cast Satan, and probably all evil angels, into it.

The chain referred to is no ordinary device of confinement known to man. No chain of forged steel could bind the power of Satan. Rather, this chain is designed and made by God.

Remember that Satan is a creature. He is neither omnipotent nor omnipresent. God is both almighty and everywhere present; thus, He can limit Satan's "creaturely" movements and activities.

Satan's Description

Within the sovereign will of God and His delegated authority, the holy angel grasps Satan and binds him (20:2). The duration of the binding is 1,000 years, the length of Christ's rule upon the earth.

In this passage, the archenemy of God, and of His redemptive program, is described in four ways. First, he is the dragon. John saw him as the great red dragon, having seven heads and ten horns (12:3, 9).

4. What aspect of Satan is conveyed by the name "dragon"?

Second, Satan is the old serpent. That title takes us back to the Garden of Eden.

5. Read Genesis 3:1–15. What characteristic of Satan is apparent in his role as a serpent?

Third, he is the Devil. This term literally means "one who casts through." He is an accuser, one who betrays.

Fourth, he is Satan. This title means "adversary." This enemy of God began his creaturely existence as Lucifer, an intelligent, beautiful angel of the cherubim class (Isa. 14:12–17). He was the angel who hovered over the throne of God (Ezek. 28:14).

6. Read Isaiah 14:12–14. What happened to change Satan from God's beautiful creature to God's enemy?

7. How might the world change with Satan and his angels incarcerated during the Millennium?

Satan's Restriction

The angel lays hold of Satan, binds him, casts him into the abyss, shuts him up, and sets a seal upon him (Rev. 20:3). No other created angel has more power than Satan; therefore, the angel could perform these functions only in the power of the Almighty God.

The ultimate purpose of the binding of Satan is the elimination of international deception during the Millennium. When Christ is ruling on the earth for 1,000 years, Satan will be inactive. The world will be marked by righteousness and peace under the sovereign authority of Christ.

Millennial Kingdom

Within evangelical Christianity there are three major millennial views. The premillennial view teaches that Jesus Christ will return to the earth to set up the Kingdom (pre: before). The postmillennial position teaches that Christ will come to the earth after the Kingdom has been established by the evangelistic and social efforts of the church (post: after). The amillennial view teaches that there will be no literal Kingdom of 1,000 years during which Christ will rule upon the earth (a: no). The amillennialist believes that the Kingdom promises given to Israel are being fulfilled spiritually in the church today.

The premillennial position is the biblically accurate position when the evidence is considered. The Millennium will be the fulfillment of the prayer taught to the disciples by Christ: "Thy kingdom come. Thy will be done, as in heaven, so in earth" (Luke 11:2). In the millennial Kingdom, the promises of the Davidic Covenant will be finalized in Christ and His reign even as they were given to Mary by Gabriel: "And the Lord God shall give unto him the throne of his father David: and he shall reign over the house of Jacob for ever; and of his kingdom there shall be no end" (Luke 1:32, 33; cf. 2 Sam. 7:16).

Duration

John mentions the phrase "thousand years" six times in this chapter (20:2–7); it appears nowhere else in the Scriptures. The millennial Kingdom, therefore, refers to the reign of Christ on earth for 1,000 years. Premillennialists assert that this time designation should be interpreted literally. Although the word "day" can be used in a non-literal sense (as in "the day of the Lord"), never are the words "month" or "year" used in that way. The addition of the numerical adjective ("thousand") further reinforces the view that these years are literal calendar years.

8. Do you have a hard time thinking about a kingdom lasting 1,000 years? Why is that?

The Rulers

John then saw thrones and their occupants (20:4). Who are these rulers? It would appear that all who share in the resurrection of the righteous dead will have some aspect of reign. Jesus promised the twelve apostles that they would sit on "twelve thrones, judging the twelve tribes of Israel" (Matt. 19:28). The first part of Revelation 20:4 ("they" and "them") definitely shows that the true church, the body of believers redeemed between Pentecost and the Rapture, will have ruling and judging authority in the millennial Kingdom.

9. How do you react when you think about being a ruler for a thousand years on this earth?

The second part of the verse shows that tribulation martyrs will be raised from the dead to reign with Christ. Since the tribulation period is an extension of the Old Testament prophetic program for Israel (Dan. 9:24–27), both Old Testament and tribulation believers will share alike in this millennial authority.

10. Revelation 20:4. How were these tribulation saints killed?

11. How would their sacrifice in the Tribulation compare to the blessings of God in the Millennium?

The Ruled

Over whom will they reign? All tribulation believers who are alive on earth when Christ returns will go into the Kingdom in their natural bodies. In their natural bodies they will have children, and their children will bear others. Believers in glorified bodies will reign over human beings who are in their natural bodies. The rule will be an extension of Christ's rule with the rod of iron.

12. How would you describe the environment into which those with natural bodies will be born?

13. Could you assume that everyone born in the Millennium will be free from sin because their environment is perfect? Explain.

Resurrections

In Revelation 20:5 John identifies the raising of the saved as the first resurrection. The usage of the adjective "first" implies a "second," namely the resurrection of the unsaved of all ages, which will occur after the millennial Kingdom at the outset of the Great White Throne Judgment (20:5, 12–14).

The two resurrections must be seen as orders, or categories, not as events in time. They are set in contrast. Those in the first are blessed, holy, exempt from the second death; they are priests and rulers with Christ. Those in the second will experience judgment, expulsion to the Lake of Fire forever, and eternal torment.

Christ was the firstfruits (1 Cor. 15:20). His resurrection guaranteed the resurrection of all men, both saved and unsaved. The saved of the Church Age will be raised at the Rapture, which precedes the Tribulation (1 Thess. 4:13–18). Both the tribulation saints and the Old Testament believers will be raised at the end of the Tribulation, when Christ descends to the earth (20:4; cf. Dan. 12:1–3). The first resurrection (of believers) occurs in three phases; whereas, all of the unsaved will be raised at the same time.

14. Read 1 Corinthians 15:17. What connection does this verse make regarding the resurrection of believers?

Final Rebellion

The first rebellion against the rule of God took place in the ideal environment of the Garden of Eden. The final rebellion will be against the reign of Christ over an earth enjoying peace and prosperity.

The 1,000 years of chained confinement will not temper the hatred of Satan toward God and His people. Under divine permission, Satan will be freed from his chains, will be allowed to leave the abyss, and will be permitted to return to earth (20:7).

Satan will go throughout the earth to deceive the nations once again. All who have been born during the millennial Kingdom will be the objects of his devious tactics. These human beings will be born with a sin nature, just as happens today. These millennial children will mature and will need to trust Christ for their salvation. Some will believe, but many will only conform outwardly to the divine rule by the rod of iron. Since their world system will be innately righteous and since there will be no satanic or demonic forces with their temptations, these unsaved will passively accept their lot in life. However, when Satan tempts them and offers them a chance to rebel under his leadership, they seize the opportunity.

15. What more could those living in the Millennium in natural bodies want? What do you suppose drives them to rebel against God?

Satan will gather these human rebels from throughout the earth into a region north of the land of Israel, known as Gog and Magog. They will advance toward Jerusalem. God will intervene directly and will destroy them with Heaven-sent fire. Satan will then be cast directly into the Lake of Fire. There he will join the Antichrist (beast) and the false prophet, and together all three will be tormented night and day forever.

16. What might it be like to observe people, whom you will have watched grow up, rebel and march against Christ?

The Great White Throne

Judgment follows death, but it does not come immediately after physical death. The Great White Throne Judgment (20:11) will not occur until after the divine suppression of the rebellion following the Millennium and just before the establishment of the new heaven and the new earth (21:1).

The contemporary universe has been polluted by the effects of human and angelic sin. Peter declared that God would burn up the present universe to make a new one (2 Pet. 3:10–13). When this fiery purging happens, the Great White Throne Judgment will occur somewhere in what is outer space to us, a site unaffected by the sin of creatures. The incarnate Son of God will be the judge upon the throne (John 5:22; Acts 17:31).

The Judged

The "dead" are the unsaved of all ages (Rev. 20:12). All strata of human society, as represented by the contrasting phrase "small and great," will stand there. There is conscious life after death for the unsaved; there will be a physical resurrection of all unregenerate men; and there will be an eternal conscious existence in the Lake of Fire.

When an unsaved person dies today, the person in his or her immaterial self (soul/spirit) goes to Hades, often translated as "Hell." The term "Hades" literally means "the unseen place," a location that no human being can see. In this dreaded place, the unsaved person is in torment, conscious, aware of loved ones left behind on earth, and totally unable to do anything about his or her spiritual relationship to God (Luke 16:19–31).

17. Why did God tell us so much about Hell and the Lake of Fire, the eventual abode of the lost?

Prior to the Great White Throne Judgment, God will call the unsaved out of Hades and unite them with a resurrected body. This is the resurrection to shame and everlasting contempt (Dan. 12:2).

Basis of Judgment

The unsaved will be judged by the Book of Life and by the books of works (Rev. 20:12, 13). The absence of a name in the Book of Life will show that there never was a time when that person passed from spiritual death into spiritual life through repentant faith in Jesus Christ

(John 5:24). Many think they are saved because of their mental or vocal profession of knowing Him; but in reality, they have never come to be known by Christ in a living, loving relationship (Matt. 7:21–23).

The books of works will give evidence of the lack of justifying faith. In addition, the quantity and quality of works will determine the degree of punishment that an unsaved person will experience in the Lake of Fire. There are degrees of sins (John 19:11), and Jesus stated that some eternal judgment would be worse for some unsaved (Matt. 11:20–24).

Results of Judgment

All those to be judged at the Great White Throne will be cast into the Lake of Fire, where they will spend eternity (20:14, 15). The first death is the event when the self-ego of a person is separated from the bodily organism. Both the saved and the unregenerate experience this physical death. The second death will be both spiritual and eternal in nature. It will occur when the unsaved person in his total being (the self-ego in a resurrection body) will be banished to the Lake of Fire. These bodies of the unsaved will be so conditioned by God as to endure eternal torment without the destruction of the material body.

18. What thoughts go through your mind as you try to comprehend the eternal state of the lost?

Making It Personal

19. What are some important lessons you learn from the rebellion of some of those born during the Millennium?

20. To whom have you witnessed since being challenged to do so in the previous lesson?

21. What do you need to set aside in order to spend time with the lost so you have opportunities to witness to them?

22. Pray for a heart of concern for those outside faith in God. Ask God for boldness to take advantage of the witnessing opportunities He provides for you.

23. Memorize Revelation 20:6.

Lesson 13

The Eternal State

Hope fulfilled! Heaven at last!

Revelation 21; 22

"I heard a great voice out of heaven saying, Behold, the tabernacle of God is with men, and he will dwell with them, and they shall be his people, and God himself shall be with them, and be their God" (Revelation 21:3).

Ninety percent of Americans believe in some sort of heavenly afterlife. Some, like actor Richard Gere, a practicing Buddhist, believe that we are experiencing heaven as we live our present lives. Gere couldn't be more wrong. God has the final word on where Heaven is and what it is like. What God has planned for believers is far beyond anything in this fallen, sinful world.

Getting Started

1. Why do you want to go to Heaven?

2. Who are you looking forward to spending eternity with the most?

This lesson will affirm that Heaven will be all that God has promised.

Searching the Scripture

John continued to be an observer of the prophetic future. He was enabled to look beyond God's program for this present earth system into eternity future.

New System in Eternity

John saw the introduction of the eternal state and the elimination of this present, temporary system (Rev. 21:1). God cursed the earth because of man's original sin (Gen. 3:17). The present heavens are even unclean in God's sight because of the effects of angelic sin and the presence of evil angels. Christ predicted that the present heaven and earth system would pass away, but how will God do it?

3. Read Revelation 21:1 and 2 Peter 3:10–13. What will happen to this old earth and the rest of the present universe?

4. Read Isaiah 65:17. What will happen to our memory of this old earth?

5. In light of the truth of Isaiah 65:17, how profitable is immersing our lives into acquiring material goods?

John next saw the holy city, which will be the dwelling place of all believers within the eternal state (Rev 21:2). The name of this city will be written on the spiritual overcomer (3:12). This is the place which

Christ is presently preparing (John 14:1–3).

6. Read Hebrews 11:13–16. How did the hope of a new, holy city affect the Old Testament believers listed in Hebrews 11?

New Blessings in Eternity

7. Read Revelation 21:3. What will be the best part of living in the holy city?

In the holy city, the redeemed will enjoy the manifested presence of God forever (21:3). God dwelt with Israel by His localized presence in the Mosaic tabernacle and the Solomonic temple (Lev. 26:11, 12; 1 Kings 8:10, 11). God the Son tabernacled, or took up temporary residence, among human beings for over thirty years (John 1:14).

8. Read Revelation 21:4. What eternal blessings does God promise believers in this verse?

9. Which of those blessings are you anticipating the most?

A third blessing is that believers in glorified bodies will view life from the divine perspective. The emphasis in 21:4 is on comfort, not on remorse. Heaven would not be Heaven if it continued to have remembrance of earth's sad experiences.

A third blessing for the child of God is that he will receive all that God has promised, because God completes everything that He has purposed to do (21:6). This fulfillment of promises involves the fourth blessing, the total enjoyment of spiritual sonship (21:6, 7). The reception of the water of everlasting life will give perpetual satisfaction. The believer-overcomer will receive the promised inheritance, which is "incorruptible, and undefiled, and that fadeth not away, reserved in heaven" (1 Pet. 1:4).

The Destiny of the Lost

10. Read Revelation 21:8. Why would God include a reminder about those suffering in the Lake of Fire at this point in His revelation about eternity in Heaven?

The destiny of the lost is set in contrast to the blessings of the saved. All who have trusted Christ as Savior will enjoy eternity in the holy city with God, but the unsaved will endure torment in the Lake of Fire apart from God. Eight deeds describe the life characteristics of an unregenerate person. Their behavioral patterns manifest the fact that they did not bring forth fruit worthy of repentance (Matt. 3:8). All rejected the gracious provision of salvation by God. For example, the fearful are those who refused to confess Christ as Savior because of their fear of human reprisal (Luke 12:8, 9).

Titles of the Holy City

One of the seven angels who poured out the bowl judgments instructed the apostle to view the holy city. The holy city is "the bride, the Lamb's wife" (21:9). The stress is on the people who will inhabit the city. Second, she is "that great city, the holy Jerusalem" (21:10). She has a divine, heavenly origin. The emphasis here is on the place.

The New Jerusalem will be the manifestation of divine glory (21:11). In past ages, God's glory was veiled in the cloud by day and the pillar of fire by night. It was manifested only within the Holy of Holies in the tabernacle and the temple. In the holy city, however, all of the redeemed will walk within the very atmosphere and environment of the glory of God.

Walls, Measurements, and Materials

The city will be surrounded by a great wall 216 feet high (21:17). This wall will have twelve gates named after the twelve tribes of Israel (21:12). Three gates will be located on each of the four sides of the wall (21:13). The wall will have twelve foundation stones with the names of the twelve apostles inscribed on them (21:14). Angels will act as sentries at the gates.

The city itself will be approximately fifteen hundred miles in length, width, and height (21:15). Opinions differ over the exact shape of the city. Most are convinced that it will be in the form of either a cube or a pyramid.

11. Try to imagine the size of the city whose base would stretch from New York to within a hundred miles of Denver. How hard is that to imagine?

The wall of the holy city will be composed of jasper. Both the interior construction and the street will be of pure gold, clear as glass crystal (21:18). The stones of the twelve foundations will be formed out of twelve different precious stones (21:19, 20). The twelve gates will be made of twelve individual pearls (21:21). The value and the beauty will overwhelm all in humble awe before the omnipotent, omniscient God Who designed and created the city. It will be an eternal, visible reminder of His greatness.

12. What would the world's grandest home look like next to this grandest of all cities?

Temple and Light

13. Read Revelation 21:22. Why will there be no need for a temple in the city?

The holy city will contain no temple, no special place of worship, for redeemed men and women will forever be in the state of constant worship in the environment of God's immediate presence. True worship "in spirit and in truth" (John 4:24) will be permanently experienced in the eternal state.

The glory of God and of the Lamb will provide the light for the holy city (Rev. 21:23). The glory of God is the outward, radiant manifestation of the beauty of His divine being. The pure, moral excellence of God will be expressed visibly within the holy city in the form of true light.

In that day, only the saved will be present in the new system, and only they will have access into the holy city (21:27).

Life

14. Why would believers not grow bored of the city after living there for a few billion years?

In the Millennium, a river will flow out of the temple and out of Jerusalem toward both the Dead Sea and the Mediterranean Sea (Ezek. 47:1, 12; Zech. 14:8). In the holy city, though, the "pure river of water of life" will flow out of the dual throne of the Father and the Son (Rev. 22:1, 2). The river will be an eternal reminder that God is the source of life and satisfaction and that the water of everlasting life was freely provided by the sacrificial death of Christ . The fullness of life will be the experience of all who dwell within the city.

The tree of life will be so large that it will span the river. It will bear twelve different fruits, one for each of the twelve months. Again, these fruits are for the constant enjoyment of life by the redeemed. Even in eternity there will be a sequence of time, as indicated by the changing of fruit each month. The leaves will provide healing for the nations as they move from the Millennium into the eternal state. Some commentators believe that the healing leaves will be used in the Millennium to prolong human life in that period.

In the eternal presence of God there will be no more curse (22:3). The curse placed upon the first creation because of Adamic sin will be removed. There also will be no night, no candlelight, and no sunlight (22:5). The redeemed will probably see only the visible person of the triune Godhead, namely Jesus Christ (John 1:18). The divine name on people's foreheads will be a sign of eternal relationship and ownership (Rev. 22:4).

15. How should knowing we are forever God's own affect our lives now?

The revelation of the prophetic future to John ended with the triumphant exclamation, "They shall reign for ever and ever" (22:5). The book of Revelation begins with a prologue, and it concludes with an epilogue (22:6ff).

Book and Blessing

The book of Revelation is both faithful and true (22:6a). It is neither symbolic nonsense nor religious myth. It is factual, accurate, and fully trustworthy.

16. Read Revelation 22:6. Why is knowing the words of Revelation are true both an encouraging and a sobering thought?

The content of the Revelation has divine origin (22:6b). The Lord God commissioned His angel to transmit the divine revelation to John.

Revelation is also a prophetic book (22:6c, 7, 10; cf. 1:3). It is history revealed beforehand. Only God knows the end from the beginning; thus, only He can tell men what will come to pass.

17. Read Revelation 22:7. What does this verse convey about the expectations placed on the reader of Revelation?

Revelation should inspire awe (22:8, 9). John was so full of wonder and gratitude for what he had seen and heard that he prostrated himself before the ministering angel. The angel then corrected the apostle to give his devotion to God alone. In like manner, when a believer properly studies this book and applies its truth, he or she will worship more.

Revelation is an open, understandable book (22:10). Daniel was a closed book, and even the ancient prophet did not understand what he had written (Dan. 12:8, 9). The book of Revelation, however, should be read, and its message can be perceived by the Spirit-taught believer.

Saved and Unsaved

The eternal destinies of human beings are fixed at the time of their death or at the second coming of Christ to the earth (22:11). People who are unjust and filthy (terms for their sinful position and practice) will remain in that condition throughout eternity. People who are righteous and holy will also remain in their acceptable standing before God. Lost individuals will not be saved in eternity, and saved individuals will not lose their salvation either.

The saved will receive rewards at the Judgment Seat of Christ, an event that occurs in Heaven immediately after the rapture of the church (22:12; 2 Cor. 5:10). In addition, the saved will have eternal access to the holy city and to the tree of life. Conversely, the unsaved will not have access to the holy city (22:15). They will be in the Lake of Fire (21:8).

Invitation and Warning

An invitation to come to Christ for salvation is pressed upon the reader. Although Christ directed John to send the book to the churches (22:16; cf. 1:4, 11), the possibility exists that a professing church member could actually be unsaved. Both the Holy Spirit and the bride, namely the true church composed of regenerate people, give a double emphasis to the invitation to come (22:17). Each reader-hearer of the book should also plead to the unsaved to come. The person who comes must recognize his spiritual barrenness and must come to Christ for the satisfaction of his moral thirst. The water of everlasting life has been made freely available to all.

A solemn warning is given to those who would tamper with the inspired, authoritative truth of the book of Revelation (22:18, 19). Only God can open, expand, and close the canon (Deut. 4:2; Prov. 30:6).

Promise and Prayer

The last words ever spoken by the resurrected, exalted Christ to any mortal man center on the imminence of His promised return (22:20). The prayer of the apostle should be the cry of every believer. The believer today should be looking up for Christ, not around for the Antichrist or inside in self-pity. May Christ come soon!

Making It Personal

18. Describe eternal life.

19. How could you demonstrate that you truly value eternal life?

20. Does your life show that you value eternal life? Explain.

21. How has this study of future events encouraged your present hope in Christ?

22. What is your biggest take away from this study?

23. Memorize Revelation 21:3.